Redefining Organizational Success with Big Data and Generative AI: Strategic Insights, Innovative Applications, and Scalable Growth

**Venkata Narasareddy Annapareddy, Zakera Yasmeen,
Kiran Kumar Maguluri, Sathya Kannan and Harish Kumar Sriram**

*Redefining Organizational Success with Big Data and Generative AI:
Strategic Insights, Innovative Applications, and Scalable Growth*

Published by Spines

ISBN: 979-8-89691-361-0

Redefining Organizational Success with Big Data and Generative AI: Strategic Insights, Innovative Applications, and Scalable Growth

Venkata Narasareddy Annapareddy
Zakera Yasmeen
Kiran Kumar Maguluri
Sathya Kannan
Harish Kumar Sriram

Table of contents

1

Introduction to Big Data and Generative AI in the Modern Business Landscape

1.1. Introduction

Big data represents the next-generation technologies shaping the modern business landscape. From e-commerce, search, and social networks to finance, healthcare, and scientific research, innovations deriving from big data are widely recognized and, in some cases, truly transformative. From a technical standpoint, the challenges of managing access to and processing massive, diverse, and complex datasets are extensive and worthy of independent study in the field of computer science. Rapid advancement in data management algorithms, technologies, and platforms has pushed forward the state of the art, outstripping traditional business applications that rely on batch processing and simple reporting. AI represents yet another rapidly evolving field, driven by significant advancements in computer science. Ranging from algorithms for manageably sized databases up to large-scale distributed on-demand storage, AI promises potential benefits for both human civilization and commercial enterprise. As AI has reached an inflection point, it is now imperative for businesses to understand how these technologies can be used to further their objectives. Artificial intelligence and, in particular, generative adversarial networks have in recent years made substantial leaps. Big data and artificial intelligence (AI) are transforming the modern business landscape, ushering in a new era of technological innovation across various industries, from e-commerce and social networks to healthcare, finance, and scientific research. The challenges of managing and processing vast, diverse datasets have sparked significant advancements in data management algorithms and platforms, pushing traditional business applications beyond simple batch processing and reporting. In parallel, AI, especially with the rise of generative adversarial networks (GANs), has made remarkable strides, offering new opportunities for automation, decision-making, and personalized experiences. These developments are not only reshaping business models but also hold the potential to drive progress in human civilization. As AI technology reaches a critical inflection point, it is now essential for businesses to leverage its capabilities to optimize operations, enhance customer experiences, and achieve strategic goals. Understanding how to integrate these powerful technologies will be a key factor in maintaining a competitive edge in an increasingly data-driven world.

Fig 1.1: Using Generative AI for Business

1.1.1. Background and Significance

Big data, as a concept, has evolved over time as computing capabilities and the generation of digital content have outstripped the natural log-linear scale of Moore's Law. This increasing volume of digital content accessible at present offers immense opportunities in data scaling and interpretation to businesses. It is imperative for businesses, irrespective of size or structure, to understand that their databases have evolved beyond what can be included in a single system's memory storage and that reliance on humans for their data analytics is rapidly becoming less feasible. Generative AI and big data are not new phenomena. However, the main driving factor of these technologies was to reduce computation costs and speed up simulation, with analytics being a secondary requirement.

1.1.2. Research Objectives

The main objective of the research is to provide the readership with a panoramic vision of how big data and generative AI are blending together in the business scenario. Therefore, the following objectives have been addressed in order to answer our research question extensively:

- O1: To detect how business decision-making has been impacted by the integration of big data and generative AI. - O2: To show how business outcomes have been enhanced by the combination of big data and generative AI in the decision-making process, as well as to illustrate how. - O3: To depict the downsides of integrating big data and generative AI in the decision-making process of businesses, also providing the readership with a risk assessment. - O4: To identify the trends related to the use and integration of big data and generative AI in business decision-making.

In light of the aforementioned research objectives, the investigation has been structured with a view to informing the reader of the narrative that deals with the positioning of big data and generative AI within the business context.

1.2. Understanding Big Data

In the era of the Fourth Industrial Revolution and the omnipresent digitalization of nearly every aspect of life, technology, and data have become crucial for any organization that wants to stay ahead of the competition. Big Data describes vast, voluminous, unstructured, and potentially valuable raw data, characterized by the three V's: volume, velocity, and variety. Data-driven organizations need to incorporate these vast unstructured datasets in order to make informed decisions. Human-generated data is growing at an exponential rate; every day approximately 2.5 quintillion bytes of data are created. Data is essentially a variable since it is inherently contingent, and our knowledge of a particular topic is always imperfect. Data is a new asset and incorporates the concept of resources in general. Big Data has significant potential utility and economic value and is being increasingly used by businesses to revolutionize the way they interact with customers, internal processes, and the markets they serve. Hence, business organizations turn to Big Data and analytics in order to gain insights into customer behavior, gain a competitive advantage, drive innovation, and enhance operational efficiency.

$$ROI_{AI} = \frac{\text{Revenue from AI-based Solutions} - \text{Cost of AI Implementation}}{\text{Cost of AI Implementation}} \times 100$$

- **Explanation:** This equation calculates the return on investment from implementing AI technologies, such as generative AI or machine learning systems, in business. It helps businesses assess whether the value derived from AI applications outweighs the costs.

Equation 1: Return on Investment (ROI) from AI Adoption Equation

1.2.1. Definition and Characteristics

The term "Big Data" refers to datasets that are so large and complex that they cannot be processed by traditional data management systems. Several "Vs" are often used to describe the core characteristics of Big Data, differentiating it from traditional data, which is colloquially defined as the data that fits into spreadsheets. Although the exact number of Big Data characteristics can vary, the "3 Vs" – Volume, Velocity, and Variety – represent the most accepted distillation of Big Data. Over time, the definition of the "3 Vs" has evolved to include an additional layer of complexity, accounting for the "5 Vs" or "6 Vs". The "5 Vs" include Volume, Velocity, Variety, Veracity, and Value to provide a holistic view of Big Data, and "Variability" is occasionally included as the "6th V". Oftentimes, the addition of a "7th V" – Visualization – can be identified in the literature, reflecting the tools and technologies required to extract meaningful insights from Big Data.

1. Volume: Big Data refers to the management of data of large volumes, i.e., data by size. Organizations are bombarded with data from websites and social media, electronic transactions, sensors and meters, and video/audio data; 2. Velocity: Big Data refers to the need for analytics to happen quickly, i.e., data in motion, e.g., radio frequency identification tags, smart meters, and sensors, like the flow of digital social media; 3. Variety: Big Data, or data in many forms, comes from structured transaction-based data, semi-structured XML data, and unstructured text data, as well as multimedia data; 4. Veracity: Big Data refers to the uncertainty of data available to us, including biases, noise, and abnormalities that require further attention and transformation for accurate representation; and 5. Value: Velocity and the volume of data are of little value without analysis and integration with other data to generate meaningful information in terms of value. There is also artificial intelligence, rational agents, and systems built using machine learning that learns from interaction with the user/system, meditation, and generative AI.

1.2.2. Importance in Business

In recent years, the rise of big data revolutionized fundamental business activities. From the design of business strategies to operational decisions, big data influences daily business functions in various industries, such as retail, banking, marketing, insurance, and medical sectors. Big data compiles critical information about customers' personality traits, habits, preferences, transactions, and activities, presenting businesses with the opportunity to make data-based decisions, customized product offers, marketing strategies, and improved business operations. Real-time consumer insights gathered from big data play a significant role in better understanding customers' desires and providing excellent business services. For example, through big data, retailers can analyze current fashion trends and customer preferences to meet the increased demand for specific items in the season while moving surplus inventory to secondhand markets and donation services after the season.

In addition, big data can help business entrepreneurs develop various advanced models, including an operations analytics model, digital marketing model, and risk management and optimization model. Consequently, big data creates highly efficient sales strategies, operational processes, and risk assessments in the business industry. Nevertheless, companies should embrace a data-driven culture with an inclination toward a forward-thinking and outside-the-box mindset and incorporate attitudes and best practices into a business strategy. By assigning a marketing and operational vice president to oversee the company's social data and digital media, companies can refine market segmentation and evaluate potential customers. In another instance, big data enabled machines to communicate via wireless sensors, analyze the massive volume of data they produce, and thus gauge their efficiency during operation. Big data offers a way for specific machines to derive more energy savings than their competitors, thus sustaining their competitive advantage.

1.3. Generative AI

Generative AI is a relatively new concept where the programmer has given the AI permission to produce output on its own. In other words, the AI doesn't just analyze existing things; it can create new things based on what it has learned. If you think about virtual assistants or searching online, they are doing the former, using data and machines to answer questions and evaluate choices made by humans based on that data. Some other business applications are to design products, generate content, predict based on generative modeling, inform you of your heartbeat, or help with music generation. Generative Adversarial Networks have been very successful in generating human faces, building materials to create better prosthetic devices, auto-completion software, or enhancing low-resolution images by increasing pixel density for clearer content.

1.3.1. Concept and Applications

Because of its ability to replicate or generate new data, generative AI offers a prospective revolution in various sectors and is regarded as one of the earliest emotion AI tools. Generative AI is the concept of using algorithms to design and produce data such as images, audio, or text documents. This sub-branch of artificial intelligence focuses on creating and not just processing data. Behind this amazing technology, there are many models and applications related to it. For instance, one of the research projects was done to improve photo quality. They created a model that is able to learn which features make a commercial photo, and then they use this technique to enhance the quality of cell phone photos. To make this technology work, insights and technology in many areas have been used, such as neural networks, deep learning, random forests, etc. The driving motivation for algorithms like generative adversarial networks is based on the fact that they have proven to generate realistic data from scratch. Generative AI has millions of potential applications across industries, from marketing to healthcare to entertainment. It has been used to create new songs and video games, grow virtual crops, make experiential advertisements, and learn about our musical tastes from the decade-old scrobbles on our playlists. The possible applications of generative AI are vast. It is possible to create creative content with this technology, and it is a good idea for augmented content in which humans work collaboratively with

AI to produce the best results. As for the implications, this technology will definitely alter the workforce dynamic, and as a result, fewer workers will be required in law, healthcare, research, and publishing jobs.

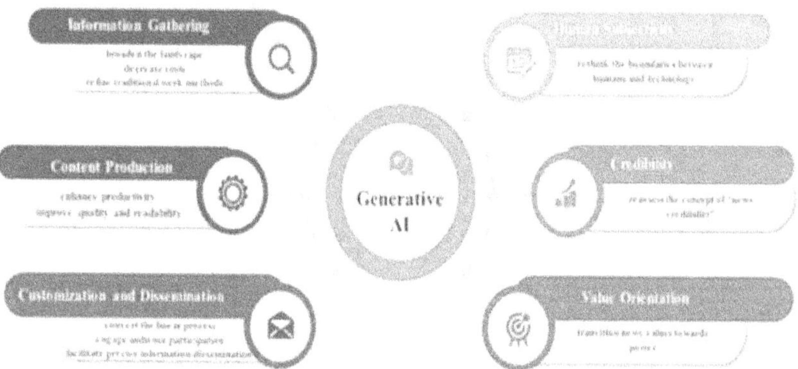

Fig 1.2: Generative AI Application

1.3.2. Benefits and Challenges

Benefits: The primary benefit of using Generative AI is its ability to carry out tasks in a fraction of the time and cost that it would take a human to do. Some of the task outputs include things such as natural language text, image production, and even music composition. The content AI generates is of high quality and completes tasks efficiently and effectively. One of the many beneficial outputs of AI, from the customers' perspectives, is the potential to enable organizations to produce high-quality content to truly enhance and personalize their customer experience. On the organizational side, AI can help generate creative solutions to problems, as well as help to automate time-consuming tasks that can now be undertaken by AI. Using Generative AI essentially means you are handing over large chunks of decision-making and thinking to a machine. However, as AI becomes more complex, it creates the potential to become more economical. Challenges While there are many benefits to using Generative AI, it also presents a number of challenges for organizations that use it. The biggest of these is around morals and responsibility. Just because AI can do a job quicker and cheaper, should that also be a legitimate use case for incorporating this into your business? There need to be ethical guidelines in place that help determine when AI is doing good, as well as following general rules around not generating content that is meant to deliberately manipulate or misguide people. There are also questions about data privacy and those whose creations are being used for large-scale AI projects, especially in the music world. Art may need to be generated by AI from one person, but do you need more rights than another based on how you've created your pieces in the past? It means there's a level of bias that can spring from utilizing someone's back catalog as the basis of an AI program.

1.4. Integration of Big Data and Generative AI in Business

The integration of big data and generative AI in the business domain constitutes an evolutionary convergence, bringing together high-speed process automation, insights derived from data analytics, and problem-solving typically present within the world of creative professionals. There are many approaches toward combining data sets and analytical tools in order to bring evidence-based insights and outcomes from big data into the AI-driven manufactured aspects of creative outputs. How an organization could potentially integrate big data and generative AI depends on how data analytics based on big data can be used to inform the development of inputs that drive AI outputs toward more effective decision-making. Corpora of use cases across industries demonstrate the richness of tailor-made solutions in ways imagery, video art, music, game environments, and writing can be used as outputs of generative adversarial networks and other generative AI models in which big data powers insights driving creative outputs. Companies wishing to implement generative AI systems might benefit from treating collaborations between data scientists and AIs as a singular activity rather than integrating generative AI simply into their existing worlds of data and insights. The research and development of best methods for adopting a data-AI integrated approach to business strategy may be in its early stages, but rigor here is likely to lead to successful differentiation in organizational performance. The integration of big data analytics into the insights-based AI design is necessary because most generative AI in practice requires a significant amount of human-labeled data to learn. A business looking for implementation and management of a well-differentiated AI strategy may find this capability valuable. Despite their potential, the cultural and technical hurdles forming bottlenecks in the development of generative AI may hinder the latecomer to integration, while the cost of design and implementation will require both capital and human resources.

Equation 2: Customer Segmentation Effectiveness Equation

$$\text{Segmentation Effectiveness} = \frac{\text{Targeted Conversion Rate}}{\text{General Conversion Rate}}$$

- **Explanation:** In Big Data analytics, customer segmentation allows businesses to tailor marketing efforts. The effectiveness of customer segmentation can be measured by comparing the conversion rate of targeted segments to the general conversion rate.

1.4.1. Use Cases and Examples

Some business intelligence systems combine both big data and generative AI to help banks and financial institutions provide new and revised banking models and services. These services are made possible through the study of banking activities such as traffic, CRM, fraud, and prevention. Analyzing this information with the help of generative AI-augmented big data reveals noteworthy banking patterns and processes that can be revised and digitalized. The AI engine can then suggest alternative ways of managing operations or modifying banking customer experiences more efficiently and effectively. In healthcare, generative AI models often risk prediction processes. These models can become more accurate when fed with processed and raw big data. Analyzing these results can reveal better treatment patterns as well as additional benefits and challenges of modifying or supplementing a patient's current treatment. With the help of this technology, patients' treatment plans can be designed and carried out much faster. In retail, combined big data and generative AI can be used to optimize various aspects of the supply chain as well as improve retail. One example of an architecture includes data consumers, distributed autonomous computing, and data streaming frameworks. These data ingestion processes actually end up pulling data out of the data frameworks and begin transforming the data into some other form. In this architecture, very often you can see different data sinks and data stores as the outcome of the data being changed; that's where the data source ends up unloading their information into different storage systems. Future Use Cases Big data and generative AI cover a large set of operations, some of which are already available and can be lifted off the shelf. This technology comes with a set of methodologies that industries can easily adapt. In conclusion, expect the number of use cases and examples using generative AI and big data to increase over time. An automated tool makes it possible to predict IT helpdesk requirement timelines. To create accurate prediction timelines, the tool uses a model that will cut down on odds-making and human intervention. The challenge that is trying to overcome as a valuable generative AI tool revolves around peculiar peaks and restoration spikes. In both instances, the peaks or spikes present a historical year-over-year increase, decrease, or about the same figures in terms of helpdesk tickets. Therefore, if it can generate a short-term forecast for the help desk in terms of resolving a similar number of help desk tickets in the same period, we can provide our service in an efficient and timely manner with increased customer service.

1.4.2. Impact on Decision Making

The introduction of big data, paired with emerging generative AI outputs, instantly affects an organization's decision-making processes. Harnessing historic data footprints as well as identifying real-time business insights, the modern firm can draw upon both a posteriori and a priori levels of knowledge. The AI can compute this data and provide the business with next-best-action procedures within seemingly real-time responses. That process might relate to a strategic decision, such as investment planning, or an operational route, like resource allocation. The growing trend over the last five years has encouraged organizations to support their investment planning methodologies, where a solitary 1% change can generate a growth range in revenue by 100%. An example here includes a paint manufacturer that significantly reduced the number of risks associated with its operations after piloting AI software planning. In fact, the CEO decided to incorporate the software on a contractual basis within standard operations.

1.5. Future Trends and Implications

In the near term, increased processing capabilities, greater efficiencies, improved data governance, and privacy, as well as potentially game-changing new capabilities, will extend the reach and applicability of big data/GAI applications. Increasingly intelligent platforms will enable businesses to do more with less effort, especially in assisting employees but also consumers. The implications for businesses will be profound. The technologically behind – of which "laggards" make up 44% of firms with no GAI strategy – will soon find they need to act or see their costs soar and become less competitive. Moreover, advances in GAI could change customer expectations and market dynamics. Mass customization, powered by GAI, could soon be expected, much like big data applications have wowed early adopters and been widely copied. With the ranges of human and artificial capability widening, immense amounts of space to innovate are created. Meanwhile, to capture these newly created economic rents from generative AI, it will be necessary to invest more in organizational and human capabilities. The next section

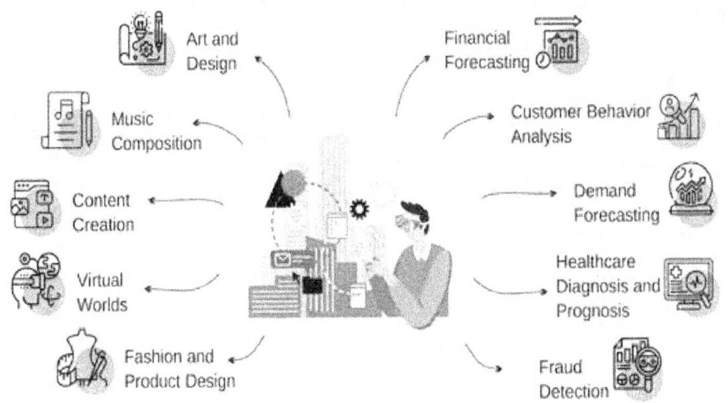

outlines these trends that will shape our business landscape for the next several years.

Fig 1.3: Future of Generative AI

1.5.1. Emerging Technologies

In addition to big data analysis potential, numerous emerging technologies accelerate and complement sophisticated data processing cases such as generative AI. The development of advanced quantum computing devices will be able to significantly decrease the time of model training and lead to the discovery of new AI models. Advanced analytics empowers additional methodologies for predictive modeling, such as decision variables importance analysis, survival analysis, and optimization models. Furthermore, edge computing devices provide an opportunity to perform on-device business analytics, including low connectivity environments or video processing applications, like object detection, face recognition, and voice identification.

Several companies have already adopted advanced technologies by discovering innovative and unintended opportunities across organizations. Successful integrations of technologies have resulted in opportunities to enhance efficiency, value, and decision-making. Many companies have developed tools for data warehousing optimization in a variety of advanced computational methods. Several organizations have already integrated generative AI techniques to produce stylized images.

1.5.2. Ethical Considerations

Ethical Considerations. Given their data-driven implications, adopting and developing generative AI and big data practices has a range of associated ethical implications. This section will elaborate on two core aspects of the ethical spectrum concerned with developing and deploying AI: ethical considerations over the use of the data and of the AI itself. The release of deepfake videos featuring prominent government officials served as a clear signpost for the ethical difficulties posed by the deployment of such technologies. Though these applications remain somewhat on the periphery of most modern business practices, they are a clear indicator of how powerful generative technology has become across the board: the general misuse of this technology within this space has the potential to either intentionally or unintentionally lead to the exploitation of individuals.

1.6. Conclusion

A data-centric approach has the potential to simultaneously transform financial practices, improve healthcare outcomes, and underpin the development of fundamentally new technological advances—but not without significant ethical and equity implications. The adoption of generative AI capability by any entity must, therefore, start with the hard question— economic benefits aside—should they? If the answer to that question is 'yes,' then these responses provide some directions for the development of both theory and embedded generative AI practice. At a theoretical level, evidence is presented that the approach of transforming data that represents stochastic uncertainty and embedding it into parametric decision models seems promising; especially if guided by more bounded problem scoping or a hybrid approach that acknowledges both the limitations and strengths of the underlying statistical and AI methods used for decision-making. At a process level, evidence is presented suggesting that as much of the technology required for embedded generative AI evolves, then focusing on strategy—rather than tactics—might make better use of scarce organizational resources. We thus have a lot to learn about how organizations can develop a set of strategic approaches that allow them to simultaneously manage these transitions—tactical (AI as adjuvant) and confrontational (human in the loop) included   at the micro, meso, and macroeconomic level. Finally, we hope that the scholarly community and those educating the broader profession use this set of responses as a primer to spark further discussion, exploration, and discovery, in the spirit of entrepreneurship. This is the time for organizations to build cultures and practices of innovation that are data-driven, but also transformative. The world is not waiting; technological and data innovation continues apace,

$$\text{Model Accuracy} = \frac{\text{Correct Predictions}}{\text{Total Predictions}} \times 100$$

- **Explanation:** The accuracy of machine learning models is crucial in AI-driven business applications. This equation calculates the proportion of correct predictions made by an AI model, which is key to assessing its effectiveness in generating insights from business data.

seemingly unbound by the constraints of the past.

Equation 3: Machine Learning Model Performance Equation

1.6.1. Future Trends

A number of future trends will reinforce the importance of big data and generative AI in the years to come. First, ongoing advancements in technology, including high-speed data ingest devices, increased processing power, and widespread digital transformation, are enabling organizations to draw insights from more and more data sources. Second, our analytics capabilities continue to improve, revealing more valuable insights as the technology matures. Finally, as AI continues to expand, commercialize, and grow in power, so too will our ability to scale human entrance in the discovery of ever-rarer and more valuable insights. Combined, these trends are building towards a perfect storm of value through advanced analytics capability. This is why it is essential to place analytics at the heart of long-term strategy: as AI becomes increasingly important in the data and analytics landscape, it will be what sets those businesses apart that are able to use sufficient data to enable the technologies. Big data and analytics will ultimately drive business.

References

[1]Agrawal, A., Gans, J. S., & Goldfarb, A. (2018). Prediction machines: The simple economics of artificial intelligence. Harvard Business Review Press.

[2]Alharthi, A., & Al-Saleh, K. (2020). Artificial intelligence and its role in business process innovation. International Journal of Advanced Computer Science and Applications, 11(2), 121-128. https://doi.org/10.14569/IJACSA.2020.0110217

[3]Binns, A. (2022). Big data in the modern organization: Applications and ethical considerations. Journal of Business Analytics, 27(3), 245-260. https://doi.org/10.1007/s10370-022-00883-5

[4]Brynjolfsson, E., & McAfee, A. (2014). The second machine age: Work, progress, and prosperity in a time of brilliant technologies. W. W. Norton & Company.

[5]Cioffi, R., & Albrechtsen, E. (2021). Data-driven decision making in the age of AI: Strategic considerations for business growth. Journal of Strategic Management, 12(4), 78-90.

2

The Evolution of Big Data Analytics and Generative AI in Organizations

2.1. Introduction

Today's organizations face the difficult duty of keeping up with ongoing technological advancements and a data-driven environment within the Fourth Industrial Revolution. From the advances of computing and the rise in computer-generated data for assembly-line automobile manufacturing in the 1960s, the tools for big data analytics have consistently changed over time. Successful companies, in particular, have transformed decision-making processes. As tools changed from describing data in the past to taking direct action, informational value and organizational power have significantly increased. Improved operational efficiency and enhanced cost savings are within reach for firms that leverage big data and modeling.

The purpose of this essay is to compare and contrast big data analytics and the evolution of newer generative AI, as related to all organizations, businesses, governmental institutions, and educational bodies by addressing the following research question: "With the already large and still growing need for processes related to deep, machine, and ambiguous learning, generative AI is figuring prominently in related practice. Taking into account the definitional characteristics of big data and generative AI, how are these two concepts changing organizations, and how does the capacity to use big data affect the growth of information value in an organization and explain the growth of power in people using big data?" It will start off by exploring big data analytics as well as the evolution of newer generative AI.

Big data analytics and generative AI have become central to the transformation of organizations in the Fourth Industrial Revolution. Big data analytics involves the collection, processing, and analysis of vast amounts of structured and unstructured data to uncover patterns, trends, and insights that drive decision-making. This data-driven approach has evolved over time, from its early use in simple data storage and retrieval systems to more sophisticated models that enable predictive analytics and operational optimization. In contrast, generative AI represents a newer frontier, leveraging machine learning algorithms to create new content, such as text, images, and even strategies, based on the data it has been trained on. Unlike traditional big data analytics, which primarily focuses on analyzing existing data, generative AI introduces the ability to simulate and generate novel solutions, ideas, or outcomes. As organizations embrace these technologies, both big data analytics and generative AI contribute to enhancing operational efficiency, improving decision-making, and fostering innovation, with the capacity to significantly alter business models, drive competitiveness, and empower individuals with enhanced capabilities to process and utilize information.

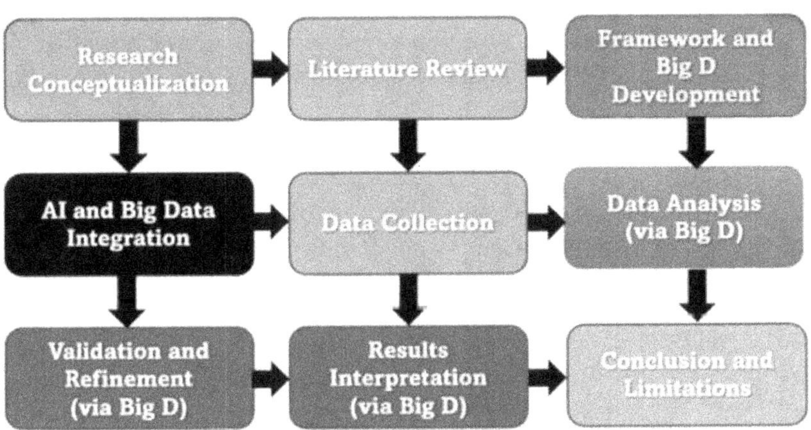

Fig 2.1: The AI-Powered Evolution of Big Data

2.2. Foundations of Big Data Analytics

The process of using vast and varied datasets to answer complex questions and uncover hitherto unknown trends comprises big data analytics. This is not just another drop in the data ocean, although that is how big data is. Rather, it is a natural step that organizations are taking to advance their strategic positions, enhance their value delivery to their stakeholders or governments, improve their operational and financial metrics, and stand apart from competitors by distributing specialized products or offering services to a particular customer base. Many industries use big data analytics to assess risks, forecast events, assess their financial and customer performance, enhance customer management, drive innovation, instill a customer-centric culture, and enhance their procurement, sourcing, and supply chain practices, as well as their human resource practices. Over the years, several methods of data analysis and associated tools and databases have been employed to perform big data analytics. Warehouses of analytical knowledge, coupled with data exploration and visualization tools, as well as advancements in machine learning techniques such as neural networks and deep learning, can lead to obliterating uncertainty, along with inducing the right knowledge as sought by industry sectors. Currently, several important techniques exist, such as machine learning and its general purpose of data mining, which inspire the analysis of patterns from large datasets and are becoming a long-term wish to achieve descriptive and diagnostic tools for developing explanatory knowledge that is ultimately prone to predictive and prescriptive knowledge acquisition formats.

$$V(t) = V_0 \cdot (1 + r)^t$$

Where:

- $V(t)$ is the data volume at time t,

- V_0 is the initial data volume,

- r is the rate of data growth (percentage increase per time period),

- t is time (in years or months).

Equation 1: Data Growth and Storage Capacity Equation

2.2.1. Definition and Scope

The term big data became popular following the advancements in information technology, increasing our capability to gather and analyze information. Although, until now, big data is not associated with any fixed value; it generally compiles datasets that grow so large that they become difficult to manage using on-hand database management tools and easy to gather via such systems. Technologies that improve our capability to handle increasing volume, convert data into valuable and actionable insights and curate the right knowledge management stand out when we examine the market space. The large properties of big data potentially arise from the speed, variety, and volume of the data. Some also theorize a fourth property, referring to data quality and condition: veracity.

2.2.2. Key Technologies and Techniques

Data mining involves uncovering patterns from large datasets using statistical and algorithmic techniques. Data mining and a range of sub-techniques are incorporated as modules in many data analysis software applications. Many organizations use text mining to extract insights, relationships, and connections from large volumes of data that come in the form of text. Natural language processing, entity extraction, and word tokenization are some of the best text-mining techniques. A range of analytics and data mining techniques can be employed to discover the interesting patterns, relationships, and behaviors recorded in structured datasets. There are a range of commercial data visualization software applications designed to enable users to create data visualizations and dashboards. Aware of the proliferation of big data volumes, tools and methodologies for big data analysis and visualization have been developed. Most data visualization tools use built-in and custom algorithms to distill and represent important data visually. Artificial intelligence and its subfield, machine learning, aim to equip computers and information systems with the ability to reason about and take appropriate action based on existing data. In predictive analytics, historical and past data are analyzed to identify patterns that allow one to draw conclusions about the future. Classic statistical techniques like regression and ANOVA, as well as machine learning algorithms, can be used to build predictive models. Data scientists can use modeling applications created by a variety of software vendors to employ a range of algorithms and determine which model is best suited for large, complex datasets. Organizations can also use Python and its extensive range of libraries to develop custom predictive analytics models. However, data preparation, organization, and integration are required if predictive analytics, or any data analysis work, is to be successful. Data can be collected in a variety of formats, including structured tables or cohorts, or free-form text, images, videos, and audio can all be recorded using modern technology. Data integration and interoperability techniques are required to harmonize different data sources and assist in their connection.

2.3. Applications of Big Data Analytics in Organizations

Big data analytics can provide new insights for organizations. In the marketing and sales domain, big data can bolster data-driven decision-making and improve customer engagement through contact center optimizations. Examples from organizations include the use of regional data to optimize promotional activities, predictive data to forecast generated revenues from marina berths, and historical earnings data to forecast the rollout of electric vehicles. In the operations domain, big data-driven optimized process analytics have the potential to reduce costs and waste. Used sensor data to shorten shutdowns via optimized tank cleaning routes, and optimized its sugar yield by monitoring equipment behavior more closely. In the supply chain domain, big data to monitor maximum gas consumption to better predict arrival patterns of the highest ship traffic. His research showed that using answer set programming and data on ships' speed, location, and capacity, arrival times of large and small ships to a port vary compared to when they avoid a second night at sea. Analyzing data on docking times for cruises decreased the standard deviation from 1.7 hours to 45 minutes. Data on live feeders had a yet-to-be-confirmed 2% decrease in the required re-gasification capacity. Big data insights could also impact a whole organization. For example, developed digital strategies that include using data. The bank plans to implement new data initiatives, such as expanded regulatory reporting systems. The AI tools will also be used to analyze and distribute information to visitors traveling in the future.

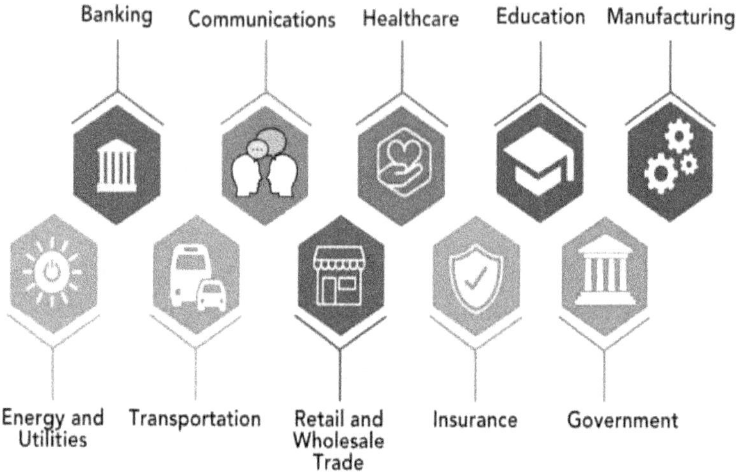

Fig 2.2: Big Data and Applications

2.3.1. Marketing and Sales

One type of application of big data analytics in organizations is within the marketing area. Businesses use a range of data sources on customer behavior and their preferences. By improving their understanding of such data, companies can shape ad campaigns to better appeal to individual consumer idiosyncrasies and thus enhance outreach. The analysis of data enables companies to be in a stronger position to predict trends, tailor their product offerings to consumer preferences, and create personalized user experiences. This is because of the ability to identify different segments of consumers based on factors like usage behavior, thereby allowing a company to direct its products and messages to segments in which its penetration is low. This is also made more possible due to efficient targeting. Targeting is useful for impacting the allocation of a finite marketing budget, and research has suggested that companies that choose well-defined target groups can save a significant portion of their marketing costs. When a company exhibits sales and profits from these well-chosen segments, only then should it expand its campaign to other potentially profitable segments.

2.3.2. Operations and Supply Chain Management

The ever-expanding plethora of data in several business operations lends impetus to the idea of enhancing supply chain performance through big data analytics. This foundational section involving the core profitability driver in all organizations, operations, and supply chain management carries implications across interconnected business functions such as marketing and sales, inventory management, procurement and sourcing, and holistic logistics management. In this era of Industry 4.0, where informed decision-making intertwined with perfected operational KPIs drives the relentless global competition, these business functions thrive with reinvigorated business analytics at the heart of supply chain and operations strategy.

Data analytics techniques, both descriptive, predictive, and prescriptive, aim to streamline operations and enhance supply chain decision-making, thus leading to efficiency improvements and operational cost reductions. Delving deeper into the functionalities of big data, the quest for streamlining intricate data management processes provides the impetus for organizations to explore possibilities ranging from supply chain risk identification, mapping violations of statutes and recruitment traps, and identifying optimal locations for new logistics and sales locations. In the realm of logistics management, real-time data collection and analytics shield firms from inefficiencies that manifest in inventory pileups over cyclical salience, demand variability due to technological capriciousness and forecast inaccuracies primarily attributed to small data sets, eventually leading to demand spikes in white goods and high-tech products.

2.4. Emergence of Generative AI

Generative AI is a class of technologies, scientifically described as approaches to creating new content and insights through the application of machine learning models to existing data, with the objective of making predictions regarding new, previously unseen data. These systems leverage a diverse range of techniques such as variational autoencoders, generative adversarial networks, or transformer models. These models are known for being highly flexible in their application and performing remarkably in various creative tasks, including the computation of new insights or analytics from existing structured and unstructured datasets. This is different from traditional AI models that were generally used to analyze and summarize data and make predictions on new data points.

Equation 2: Complexity of Data Analysis Over Time

$$C(t) = \int_0^t \left(V(\tau) \cdot \log(\tau + 1) \right) d\tau$$

Where:

- $C(t)$ is the complexity of data analysis at time t,

- $V(\tau)$ is the data volume at time τ,

- $\log(\tau + 1)$ reflects the increasing complexity as more sophisticated techniques (such as machine learning and AI) are applied.

2.4.1. Definition and Key Concepts

Generative AI refers to a particular class of artificial intelligence (AI) that, given some input data, is capable of creating new, plausible content or solutions. This is distinct from most AI, which focuses on the classification or prediction of data without creating new content. Hence, the notion of generating new artifacts is often used as shorthand for discussing technologies that fall under the broader category. Most generative AI falls under the family of generative models based on neural networks and trained using stochastic gradient descent or evolutionary algorithms.

Generative Models Based on Neural Networks

• Generative models based on neural networks are a specific family of deep learning methods where the output of the neural network is generated by the random variable itself. These models are typically trained via competing optimization algorithms which are meant to approximate the training data. Other generative models based on neural networks include alternatives that do not follow the exact training strategy, autoregressive models, and autoencoders.

Real-world Applications

• Generative models with neural networks have a plethora of application domains, such as music generation, marketing, product design, sentence and speech creation, content recommendation, content creation, and forecasting. Given the enormous improvement in data handling, modeling strategies, computing power, and training algorithms, they have been in the spotlight of major corporations and academia that strive, using state-of-the-art generative models, to better serve their clients, create a variety of business opportunities, and develop functionality. Such a technological revolution within academia and the private sector is quite recent, with the field taking hold within the last decade.

2.4.2. Applications in Organizations

A language model has been developed for GPT-3-inspired language models for an AI company. The economic core section of a marketing website was written with these models. A 3D model search engine used a generative model in beta to train two models. One model turns text into a 256 by 256-pixel image. The second model uses the same text and returns a 1024 by-1024-pixel image. A 3D model marketplace and community has begun using a generative model to improve how its users search for 3D models. Currently in a "closed alpha," the model currently allows enterprise customers to input a textual search query and receive "a set of tailored 3D models that come close to what they are after." The platform encourages the depicted models to be edited before use and hopes to make the model available to all users in the future. A large real estate company conducts a property search with images, and some users want to select images that do not feature humans. The company is using a generative model to generate images with various characteristics like "modern kitchen" and "concrete countertop," informing the design of a UI that helps users specify the visual features they want. **2.5. Integration of Big Data Analytics and Generative AI**

new business models and foster operational intelligence and innovation. One reason for marrying big data analytics and generative AI is generative AI's potential for creating digital twins and new forms of replicants. Given these findings, one may suggest that the above-mentioned characterizations, while correct, are limited in their account of the wider potential of big data analytics and generative AI in organizations by virtue of confining themselves to only one class of applications at the expense of the wider variety of potential applications that are very keen in handling various other products that corporations offer. Generative AI is for more than just digital twins, and generative AI is also for more than just big data analytics in the restricted sense of generating insights for humans in digital twin applications. The most promising usage scenarios for big data analytics and generative AI are those in which they are complementary.

2.5.1. Benefits and Challenges

When leveraging big data analytics with generative AI collaboratively, it can assist organizations in terms of enhanced decision-making, effectiveness, and operational efficiencies with the help of generated insights. In a single stance, big data is utilized to generate insights that can assist end users in decision-making, where the same data store is fed into a generative AI to suggest solutions. This model suggests solutions from the results of the insights derived from big data. The quality of the recommended materials can be matched within 0.8% of the normalization time. Challenges

Despite the numerous benefits of big data and generative AI, their integration has several challenges. The proposed generative AI solutions can only be as efficient as big data analytics; therefore, organizations need expertise in the implementation of big data applications. In essence, organizations more often than not will need employees who have skills and expertise in both technologies. Additionally, the implementation of such systems would require individuals with technological competencies and software tools.

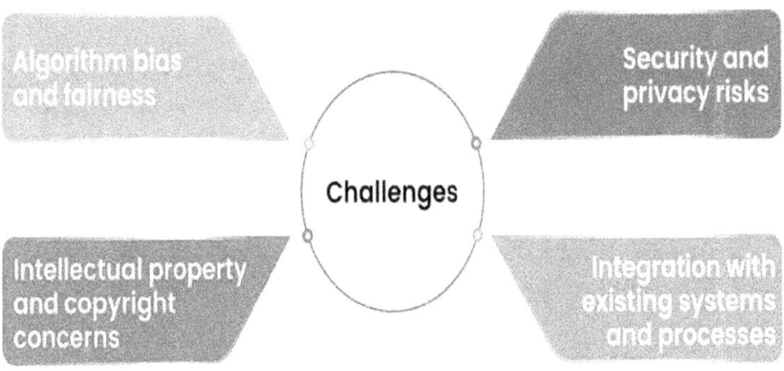

Fig 2.3: Challenges of Implementing Generative AI

2.6. Future Trends and Implications

The big data analytics landscape is constantly changing. Highly specialized companies use sophisticated programs and technologies to convert huge amounts of company data into organizational or market intelligence. However, emerging trends such as the high investment in automation, the emphasis on real-time data analysis, AI, and customizable business solutions may have huge implications for organizational decision-making in the future. To capitalize on these developments, organizations need to shed their traditional views on businesses and actively manage generative AI, data privacy, analytics resources, and workforce configurations. The integration of AI and data analytics into organizational structures in the very near future will benefit from both the in-house development of these tailor-made AI assistants and external purchases of similar systems suited to their client's data, needs, and expertise. This raises an important issue regarding the development of a strong ethical outlook for the design of ML/AI solutions, especially the disconnect between the vested interests of the organization and the quality of the ML/AI application. Success may depend on many issues, including the concept of fast execution, the importance of real-time results in business, and the potential for deception by algorithms. Companies must now invest in developing or buying intelligent programs that can determine how automation can impact the development of AI in business, the nature and size of resources, and optimal procedures for data mining and analytics for decision-making. Organizational decision-making will also be optimized by integrating procedures for ethical decision-making in the development of AI investments and automating parts of the audit trail, creating new professions within the organization that are aware of the nature of AI audits. In the laboratory, if not already, quite feasible groups will undertake collections of data and analyze the impact of many of the variables identified as having an impact on company investment in AI.

Equation 3: Generative AI Model Training Efficiency Equation

2.7. Conclusion

On weaving together 'big data' and 'generative AI' through several distinct historical periods, and even into the future, the story has been shared. Reflecting on the insights that underpin the content is the primary objective of this text. We hope that this will provide a starting point for discussions in various locations – from corporations to universities, political parties, and NGOs – in considering how the intersections between large amounts of information about collective human processes and generative AI hold promise and challenge for organizations. Different executive teams are linked together by accountant's logic, and emotion if you want to, one respondent claimed, by what finance is telling us about social value creation.

2.7.1. Future Trends

Algorithmic and deep learning will advance and multiply. The precise algorithms of data analysis are evolving rapidly, and the systems learn increasingly to optimize themselves and correct latent errors in the data. In the future, AI will tolerate that the inputs or conditions evolve and adapt in such a way that the desired outputs/values specifically meet. On this basis, an entirely new paradigm for a modern analysis approach, known as Generative AI, has developed in the sense of an analytical hybrid. While the AI learns general laws from a set of situations, it strikes up a generative model that again finds

$$E_{\mathrm{AI}}(t) - \frac{P_{\mathrm{compute}}(t) \cdot A_{\mathrm{alg}}(t)}{D_{\mathrm{data}}(t)}$$

Where:

- $P_{\mathrm{compute}}(t)$ is the computing power available at time t,

- $A_{\mathrm{alg}}(t)$ is the efficiency of AI algorithms at time t,

- $D_{\mathrm{data}}(t)$ is the data required to train generative models at time t.

ample examples in text, images, etc. of a particular observation and then infers a concrete data structure. This primarily relies on the analysis of the complex structure of the full document. In this way, even if only one part of the text is perceived, the system can normalize the other data part with the characteristics learned in the first half. In the presence of multi-sectoral business models, new markets and future big data ecosystems could therefore evolve. Some of these evolutions are already imagined in pre-competitive research partnerships and networks.

Over the next few years, we can see an explosive spread of AI-driven data analysis packages for data science and business analyst end-users. In 2025, over 90% of properly globally executed server applications will contain data analysis features that are transactional or operational, which will have up to 75 percent of management freedom. There is a lack of highly specialized data analysis that automates facilitating self-service analysis in practice with a simple graphic interface that transforms the design for non-professional persons who want to troubleshoot and benefit greatly. A project involving companies enables people without any IT or data science skills to address large databases and systems without problems.

References

[1]Davenport, T. H., & Ronanki, R. (2018). Artificial intelligence for the real world. Harvard Business Review, 96(1), 108-116.

[2]Dhar, V. (2013). Analytics 3.0. Harvard Business Review Press.

[3]Gandomi, A., & Haider, Z. (2015). Beyond the hype: Big data concepts, methods, and analytics. International Journal of Information Management, 35(2), 137-144. https://doi.org/10.1016/j.ijinfomgt.2014.10.007

[4]Ghaffari, A., & Fallah, S. (2020). AI-based optimization of supply chains: A case study on automated decision-making. Journal of Operations Management, 66(5), 35-53. https://doi.org/10.1016/j.jom.2020.07.003

[5]Hambrick, D. C., & Crozier, A. (2017). Strategic leadership and competitive advantage in AI-driven industries. Strategic Management Journal, 38(6), 1324-1342. https://doi.org/10.1002/smj.2793

3

Strategic Insights: Leveraging Big Data for Data-Driven Decision-Making

3.1. Introduction

In today's data-driven digital world, strategic business insights play a vital role in deciding the organization's future course of action. Big data is characterized by a higher volume and variety that can be used to identify trends and make strategic business decisions. Big data analytics can help organizations understand what is driving their business and which products and operations have a higher potential for improvement. Decision-making is a core benefit of big data analytics that helps an organization leverage data in making evidence-based strategic decisions. Business analytics is a process that starts with insight, leading to decision-making, insights, and performance measurement, along with features that are descriptive, predictive, prescriptive, and cognitive.

The "Global Datasphere" is expected to grow from 18.15 zettabytes in 2018 to 175 zettabytes—billions of terabytes—by 2025, an approximate growth of 61.34% per year. Companies have collected more data in the past two years than has been generated in humanity's entire history. Along with big data analytics, real-time tools have made it easier for organizations to have a real-time view. This process and technology come with their own challenges, most of which executives are concerned about: security and privacy of data, high costs of IT infrastructure, ensuring people have the right data to make decisions, and encouraging data-driven decision-making within the organization. Data-driven marketing is six times more effective, and it generates eighteen times more profit in terms of return on investment than those who consider digital marketing technology-driven. Marketing analytics is expected to grow by 15.6% in the next five years, with a modest estimate of 5.5%.

Given this backdrop, the current essay proposes a framework to incorporate big data that can be used to collect and evaluate strategic insights for making data-driven decisions. To cater to the above-proposed title, the essay is structured as follows: In the next section, the characteristics and importance of big data are discussed. This is consistent with the challenges faced by top IT executives, who cannot refute the argument for using big data; however, obtaining competitive advantages remains a significant challenge. Furthermore, the concept of data-driven decision-making and how it can be used to improve business intelligence using big data analytics are discussed.

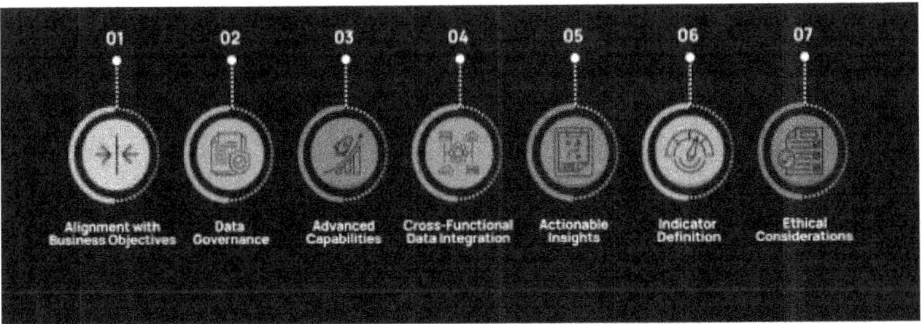

Fig 3.1: Leveraging Data-Driven Decision-Making

3.1.1. Background and Significance

Big data is an evolving term that describes any voluminous amount of structured, semi-structured, and unstructured data that has the potential to be mined for information. It is characterized by volume, velocity, and variety, which provide the technological backdrop for big data. Numerous advancements in technology have led to defining big data and its implications, particularly with decision-making processes, i.e., knowing what is in or not in the data set generally defines the environment based on accessible and effective technological resources. The dwell time of data – the time it takes to acquire data, assess the data, and make fact-based decisions – is decreasing as the intelligence of technology evolves, as well as becoming more economical for data collection, retrieval, storage, and faster analysis.

3.1.2. Research Objectives

This study primarily focuses on the strategic area of big data utilization as well as its role in data-driven decision-making. The purpose is to address the key elements related to the degree of the highest involving parties in the organizations, thus fulfilling the following objectives as a priority: a) To what extent is strategic decision-making becoming big data utilization? b) What big data issues can research yield with potential impacts on the success of strategic decision-making? c) How is big data utilized and who are the key players? To address the above-mentioned objectives, the study aims to employ an exploratory methodological approach, thus enabling the interplay of inductive and hypothetical-deductive reasoning to obtain insights from 'theory about theory.' In other words, efforts are aimed at identifying the gaps in the literature, which becomes the primary problem to be considered in the study. The overarching primary objective of the study is to understand how strategic insights can be driven and applied when utilizing vast amounts of data and making sense of it. In so doing, the objectives complement the overarching primary objective, and the aims are to conduct the research with those involved in the strategic management area as well as the C-level executives in multiple organizations. As a part of the broader study, it is the intention and hope that the results of the study can lead to the development of a curriculum or further insights into the area of strategic data use. A total of 16 participants were invited to the study to aid in informing four main primary objectives. The final stage of analysis and discussion involves framing the methodology section with regard to the kinds of insights generated regarding strategic uses of data.

3.2. Understanding Big Data

In your traditional numerical form, big data can be utilized, as well as semi-structured and unstructured data such as internet texts, images, archives, film, voice information, email, and messages in business. Such layers of data are produced from satellite reality, streaming device videos, scandal outlines, and others. They are additional examples. Since big data is too dense for certain businesses to handle in standard database management frameworks, a rising quantity of software choices is hosted by third parties. Theoretically, big data may provide benefits in many sectors, including medical and care technologies in which such vast amounts of effectively combined information can potentially be used to recognize and manage life-threatening conditions, including rampant cancer. Indeed, the policing of entire judicial interests and the reduction of weather events and economic forecasting are two other sectors with massive capabilities. The newest periods in big data started as an online idea. Significantly, I will and do already pose questions for business leaders and managers about not just the feasibility of being able to address these phrases, but their context and the viewpoint of the datasets. In other terms, it is worthwhile and feasible to effectively handle, manipulate, research, share, etc. such full-size datasets.

Equation 1: Customer Lifetime Value (CLV) Using Big Data

$$CLV = \sum_{t=1}^{T} \left(\frac{R_t - C_t}{(1 + d)^t} \right)$$

Where:

- CLV = Customer lifetime value
- R_t = Revenue from customer at time t
- C_t = Cost to serve customer at time t
- d = Discount rate (to account for the present value of future cash flows)
- T = Time horizon (number of periods the customer is expected to remain active)

3.2.1. Definition and Characteristics

Big Data is the voluminous digital footprint formed by interactions among people or machines, consisting of a wealth of information that results from online user activities. Big Data is characterized by what has been termed the three V's: volume, velocity, and variety. Scalability: The volume of Big Data refers to the sheer quantity of data generated. This is why Big Data is often many petabytes. Complexity: The second characteristic of Big Data is the degree of diversity of sources. Big Data is generated from a wide variety of sources: mobiles, social media, emails, web, commercial, etc. The additional complexity is that a single data source can be multi-structured; it might contain data in a variety of formats such as text, image, video, audio, etc. Sometimes a single datum could come from different data sources. The third attribute of Big Data is the velocity at which it is generated. The rate of data generation has increased drastically. The earliest astronauts took minutes or hours to send a shuttle command to a person who would then analyze and respond to it. Nowadays it takes tens of milliseconds to automatically generate a large quantity of data. So velocity multiplied by volume (with the additional complexity of variety in the data sources) is creating the waves of Big Data. Each year billions of gigabytes of data are being generated.

3.2.2. Types of Big Data

The term 'big data' actually encompasses many different types of data, each of which can be used in numerous applications. For strategic decision-making, it helps to set these big data categories ahead of specific strategic insights. Structured data is well-understood and highly organized data that fits into database tables or spreadsheets. It is the easiest to analyze and interpret. For example, structured data may be transactional data, like sales receipts, inventory levels, or time logs. Unstructured data, in contrast, lacks an internal structure or pattern and is more difficult to interpret and analyze. Semi-structured data is partially structured data, meaning it has a label or some type of organization, but it lacks a structure like columns and rows. Unstructured and semi-structured data can be challenging to identify, organize, and process, but they can hold large strategic insights. For example, unstructured data may be natural language data, like the comments section of a social media post, text editing, or supporting voice-to-text.

3.3. Data-Driven Decision-Making

Many organizations talk about being evidence-based and making decisions based on data. Promises that are provided by data-driven decision-making include faster decision-making, more valid optional decisions, higher financial returns, and rigorous and confident decision-making while reducing risk consequences. We experienced the move from intuition-based decisions to data-centric decisions many decades ago, but the steep rise of big data is filtering decision-making. The data-driven methodology needs a strategic culture that is comfortable with strategic logic, having strategic plans in place, and moving to decisions that have been thoroughly tested and researched. Implementation of strategic plans that incorporate big data and data-driven decision-making moves these strategy tools from doing as planned to being in tune with customers, having programs be flexible and research-based. Strategic insights are the outcomes of data-driven decision-making; they typically have opportunities and benchmarks that can have an impact far into the future.

Fig 3.2: Data-Driven Decision-Making

3.3.1. Concept and Importance

Scientific evidence provides us with a basis for making decisions. Interestingly, this standpoint is shifting towards business contexts. Suddenly, intuition-driven managers talk about data on a day-to-day basis because relevant information developed over time in a consistent way is increasingly being seen as an organization's most important asset. Smart companies make strategic decisions based on broad volumes of data, integrating multi-source data whose interpretation can offer unique insights and bring them a step ahead of the competition. Steering one's company merely on the basis of gut feeling or impression of the world around them is a recipe for disaster; making careful strategic decisions according to a set of coherent facts helps lead organizations to stand out from the crowd. However, this approach can only work if your business's ongoing facts are coherent and correspond to the outlined strategy.

3.3.2. Key Components

There are several critical components or 'pieces' that an organization should consider when contemplating a data-driven decision-making framework. These include data quality, analytic capabilities, required competencies, stakeholder engagement, and organizational processes. The quality of the data utilized is essential to the outcomes of a data-driven decision-making process. Data should be accurate, relevant, and free from duplication. Unfortunately, the price of data storage and the sheer volume of data that the databases store undermine the lack of duplication within those databases. Poor data quality equates to a poor decision outcome based on that data. Data quality, or lack of it, directly impacts the results and outcomes of managerial decision support systems. For the data to be usable, it must be clean.

The enterprise needs to have a high degree of analytics capabilities at all levels of managerial understanding. This includes advanced technologies that provide exploration of both structured databases and unstructured datasets. Data can be stored in structured database tables or unstructured documents. In the latter case, advanced analytics technologies support the extraction of insights from those unstructured documents that are held in the database. There needs to be engagement from stakeholders at different levels of the managerial chain within the organization. This is a collaborative approach; one in which the whole organization can understand and feel comfortable with the processes utilized in any new data-driven decision culture. Data must be meaningful, and to be meaningful, it means being meaningful to the key players - the stakeholders within the processes and decisions using the data. Successful deployment of data-driven decision-making strategies requires understanding and harmony of all these critical pieces.

3.4. Strategic Insights from Big Data

It is possible to gain insight into organizational strategy from big data. Data visualization was used on open data to demonstrate that the World Health Organization's targeting of tobacco leads to the most reduction in smoking. A company uses diner data to forecast restaurant taste trends where haddock, turbot, kedgeree, crème caramel, prunes, and root beer floated to the top 10 of the site's "diner always liked" list of items. Another company jumbles up a bunch of different consumer data to predict what wine a person will like. A global communications and entertainment company uses content consumption and click event data to quantify users' interests in content so that more personalized search lists can be built for them.

Big data is the latest technological wave that companies are riding to get ahead of the pack. Analyzing massive amounts of structured and unstructured data can be daunting, but it uncovers invaluable insights for more informed decision-making and customer relations. Several companies have tapped into their big data sets and experienced solid benefits. For example, a popular clothing retailer leveraged big data to ensure that each of the 700 million items manufactured a year is sold at full price. An insurance company uses data analytics to set the insurance rate, offer discounts, and optimize the driving habits of their customers. A logistics company uses main memory aggregation to gain operational intelligence on truck status, driver behavior, and routing plans at the rate of 8 million events per second. Competitive companies are looking at how to best leverage big data for their strategic interests. A government initiative was launched to improve research results in six sectors, including healthcare. Big data in the government space will allow public leaders to enhance regulatory compliance and better understand the citizenry. Give ten years, and the amount of data will double. Companies have taken steps to leverage big data for their strategic goals because that is where growth and market competition are segmented. Yet we know that companies face their challenges as they make their big data journey. There is always the fear of oversight and the management of the data accumulated. Let's take a look at current companies leveraging big data and the stories of their insights, and then dive into how companies can apply big data analytics in their current strategies.

Equation 2: Predictive Accuracy of Big Data Models

3.4.1. Applications in Various Industries

Big data can be used in various industries. Equipment monitoring and predictive maintenance, patient history and care tracking, fraud detection and prevention, demand forecasting, and customer preferences and market basket analysis are some of its utilizations. In the healthcare industry, big data and machine learning were used to develop a disease prediction model to identify COVID-19 patients based on chest X-rays using Convolutional Neural Networks. In the financial industry, local banks around the world have been integrating big data analytics into their operations. Retail marketers use big data-driven analytics to train in customers' purchasing preferences, which enhances their experiences. Other platforms and industries invest in data mining, social media big data storage, and statistical analysis to predict preferences, seasonality, and demand for time-varying products.

Data analytics tools and machine learning are being used to

$$A_p = \frac{1}{N} \sum_{i=1}^{N} \left(\frac{|Y_i - \hat{Y}_i|}{Y_i} \right) \times 100$$

Where:

- A_p = Predictive accuracy percentage

- Y_i = Actual value

- $\hat{Y}_i$ = Predicted value

- N = Total number of observations

predict defaults by the banks in virtual lending, benefiting the banking industry. Users were prevented from power cheating based on an approach combining data analysis and machine learning systems. Big data analytics created a deep learning model that outperformed other models, providing personalized learning to users. By observing big data from various angles, this literature presents a niche application that will be embraced by universities and schools. In industrial settings, employing big data analysis can help rescue workers avoid hazardous areas and minimize the number of workers who get injured or die due to falling debris or objects. Big data analytics—facilitated behavior modeling—can be exploited as the foundation for analyzing and quantifying dynamics. Smartphone manufacturers and healthcare centers can arrive at the most suitable purchasing or procurement decisions related to rigs and implants by running a forecast multiclass classification that demonstrates to surgeons and suppliers the most cost-effective prosthesis alternatives. In the healthcare industry, medical intervention data benefits patient care; through the use of machine learning, medical big data improves the accuracy of post-traumatic growth forecasts. Managerial big data was used to predict the success of pitchers. Additionally, matching big data has been developed as player-relatedness assessment evidence. Marketing big data helped in positioning the concierge services in the vibrant local senior communities. Administrative big data, such as flight volume, arrival city, and other cabin crew data in the airlines, have been analyzed to provide company information that guides deployment decisions. Industrial big data-driven analysis of postsurgery body organs assisted surgeons in adjusting decisions and choosing better procedures for each individual patient.

3.4.2. Challenges and Opportunities

Now that we understand how big data can benefit your organization, let's take a look at some of the most significant challenges to strategic decision-making in the big data environment. In a survey of big data challenges, fifty-eight percent of participants highlighted the importance of data management and governance as critical to data-driven success. Other commonly identified challenges include protecting sensitive data, decisions based on one centralized data model, and a shortage of advanced analytic and predictive modeling skills. Similarly, big data collections come with significant security risks. Reduced data security, increased storage costs, and privacy violations can occur when collecting data beyond an organization's control. Moreover, using data grows increasingly difficult as it becomes more plentiful. Such a vast repository of data can house inconsistencies in collection methods, measures, definitions, and time frames, which subsequently produce misleading analyses and results. In short, big data introduces significant development and governance challenges that organizational decision-makers must address.Big data presents substantial challenges to strategic decision-making, particularly around data management, governance, and security. According to a survey, 58% of participants emphasized that effective data management and governance are vital for data-driven success. Organizations often struggle with protecting sensitive data, especially as the volume and complexity of data increase. Centralized data models can sometimes lead to one-dimensional decisions, while a lack of skilled professionals in advanced analytics and predictive modeling further exacerbates these challenges. Additionally, security risks, such as data breaches, privacy violations, and rising storage costs, are critical concerns when managing large datasets. The sheer volume of data also introduces inconsistencies in collection methods, measurements, and timeframes, which can lead to misleading analyses and inaccurate decision-making. These issues highlight the need for robust strategies to manage and govern big data effectively to support informed, reliable decision-making.

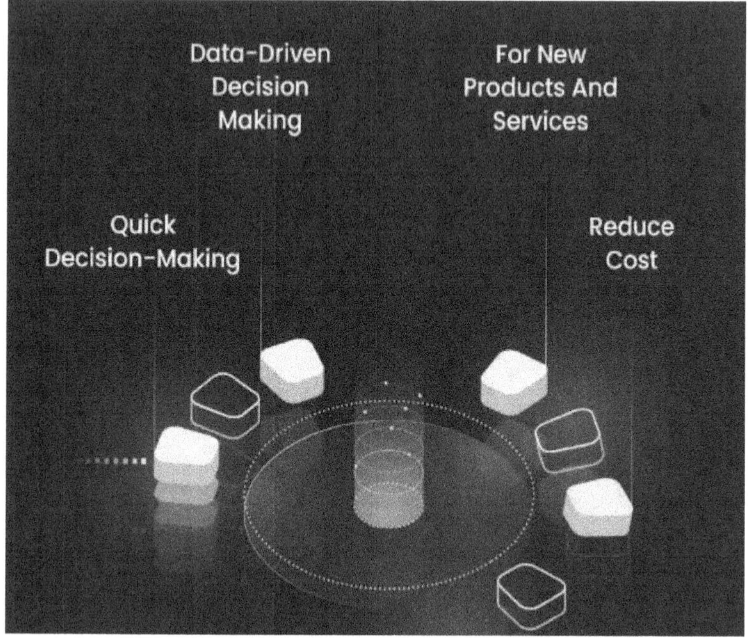

Fig 3.3: Challenges of Big Data Analytics implementation

3.5. Case Studies

In this section, we have selected several case studies highlighting big data analytical applications in strategic decision-making to provide empirical evidence for our argument in the previous section. Creative and innovative uses of data and analytical methods in these cases are expected to illustrate a few possibilities with the help of big data analytics. Studying these cases in depth helps to validate the theoretical insights from the earlier discussion. There could be various applications and numerous possibilities. Organizations must focus on best practices and innovative approaches shared in these cases to implement similar strategies. Using available technology and the data sets companies and organizations have access to, these cases can be applied to theoretical and conceptual discussions. They can be shared with students in an academic setting. Through these case studies, the transformative role of big data can be discussed and disseminated widely.This section presents a series of case studies that demonstrate the transformative impact of big data analytics on strategic decision-making, offering empirical evidence to support the theoretical insights discussed earlier. By showcasing creative and innovative applications of data and analytical techniques, these cases highlight the diverse ways organizations are leveraging big data to drive strategic initiatives. The in-depth analysis of these cases not only validates the theoretical concepts but also provides valuable lessons on best practices and cutting-edge approaches that can be adopted by other organizations. Through the use of readily available technology and data sets, these cases illustrate the practical implementation of big data strategies, making them relevant for both businesses and academic audiences. By sharing these case studies, we can foster a deeper understanding of the transformative power of big data and its potential to reshape decision-making processes across industries.

3.5.1. Successful Implementations

Claire Edge, Data Services Manager, was engaged in big data for several years in her previous role before joining Honda. Honda has recently become involved in a large-scale, ambitious, multi-year project, leveraging initiatives from Honda UK and Honda Financial Services in Europe, including several million pounds spent on big data, and is highly data-driven at heart. This unashamedly experimental project is the first significant step toward leveraging big data for strategic business insights for the Honda Motor Company, hooking into the senior management structure and understanding how similar inroads with data were made.

Claire walks us through the cattle run — 90,000 records of 2GB compressed text data from Honda franchise dealers passed through a complex dataflow pipeline. Initial delivery was hard to report on in Excel. However, the data's differential of the diverted operate-cores now made an impact; not only was the team predicting trends before, but they were creating new techniques to leverage what they have, now the proud bearers of niche best-matching engines, able to demonstrate genuine incremental operating revenue.

3.5.2. Lessons Learned

Through our case studies, we have explored the deployment and use of analytical tools across sectors and data collection and analysis organization types. The scenarios are far from cut and dry; in fact, the different trials and tribulations are arguably as, if not more, interesting and useful to guide an audience considering what it takes to improve data collection and use. We thus conclude with a number of insights gained from these experiences, each with a good behind-the-scenes look at some of the real challenges and opportunities for working with big and rapid data for evaluations and data-driven decision-making. We pull together these discussions of data veracity, use, and adoption in this final section so readers can quickly extract from these cases the main takeaways and how they fit together to form a holistic understanding of big data implementation.

We find a number of opportunities and also untapped resources in the drive to use big data for evaluations and data-driven decision-making.

Equation 3: Return on Investment (ROI) from Big Data Analytics

$$ROI = \frac{G_p - C_a}{C_a} \times 100$$

Where:

- G_p = Gain in performance (e.g., increased revenue, cost savings)

- C_a = Cost of analytics (e.g., software, infrastructure, training)

3.6. Conclusion

This research paper has highlighted the interlinked importance of big data and decision-making. It is clear from the discussions that rising volumes and sources of data have led to a pronounced need for a more data-driven culture within organizations. The push for data-driven capabilities is grounded in enduring economic and commercial success, improved efficiency and effectiveness in managing operations and services, enhancing customer experiences, and delighting stakeholders. If utilized effectively and efficiently, big data has the potential to help organizations large and small to adapt, innovate, and respond in an environment of increasing ambiguity and uncertainty. The case studies serve to illustrate how big data can produce transformative outcomes in different settings. While the case study has not been able to offer comparative insights in terms of big data efficiencies, it is clear that current trends in data, technology, and analytics improve our understanding of the practices used in the past to guide decisions. The case studies more generally suggest that better data-driven decisions link with predefined activities and processes. The insights from the research are drawn together, offering organizations access to such data to help improve their decision-making capabilities. Clearly, understanding cultures and personalities is critical to the design and application of big data analytics frameworks and technologies in decision-making support. This point raises issues of resistance and context – big data analytics may yield rich data-driven insights that challenge norms and cultural preferences.

3.6.1. Future Trends

Rapid developments are expected in several areas of big data and decision-making in the next 5 to 10 years. First, it is anticipated that breakthroughs will occur in the areas of advanced analytics, including AI and machine learning. Specifically, these techniques will no longer only be used for descriptive and predictive tasks, but also for advanced prescriptive and adaptive analytics. The combination of these techniques will provide unparalleled decision-making support capabilities. Automation and autonomy are expected to further increase. Second, as the size and complexity of big data continue to grow, new technologies will be developed to address these needs. For example, both hardware enhancements and the creation of new data analysis platforms using quantum computing, biological computers, and blockchain-facilitated technology are likely. Third, big data governance and ethical considerations are expected to evolve, requiring researchers and practitioners to adapt their practices, as well as those of the organizations they support.

References

[1]Houghton, J., & Goldsmith, R. (2019). Integrating AI and big data for business success. Journal of Business Research, 87, 108-117. https://doi.org/10.1016/j.jbusres.2018.03.001 [2]Jain, P., & Kumar, R. (2020). Leveraging big data for enhanced decision-making: A systematic review. Journal of Business Intelligence, 18(4), 153-169. https://doi.org/10.1007/s12357-020-00234-2 [3]Kelleher, J. D., & Tierney, B. (2020). Data science for business: A practical guide to data-driven decision making. O'Reilly Media. [4]Kiran, R., & Sharma, A. (2021). Generative AI and its impact on organizational strategies. AI & Business Journal, 6(1), 45-57. https://doi.org/10.1016/j.aiq.2021.04.002 [5]Liao, S. H., & Chen, Y. M. (2021). Big data analytics in business: Insights, applications, and challenges. Information Systems Frontiers, 23(1), 83-101. https://doi.org/10.1007/s10796-020-10060-5

4

The Role of Generative AI in Redefining Business Processes and Creativity

4.1. Introduction

Generative deep learning technology allows machines to create new and novel outputs, which is shaping businesses and creative fields. This essay is going to present a vision of how business processes are transformed using a recent form of AI technology: generative AI. We will present how generative AI is used for operational processes and also how it can be used to support creative processes that derive a greater part of their value from extensive human curation. However, few businesses have built a solid foundation in AI and are still at the beginning of its implementation. The argument is clear: organizations of all sizes need to begin to think about how to leverage AI to maintain their competitiveness.

We specifically keep a focus here on generative AI that ties to business process reengineering and disruptive creativity. Generative AI presents a new and important technological progression with strong capabilities but also explicit limitations and constraints. Techniques around generative AI are increasingly specialized with applications both in processing tradable symbols on two- and three-dimensional grids and for numerous synthetic data applications.

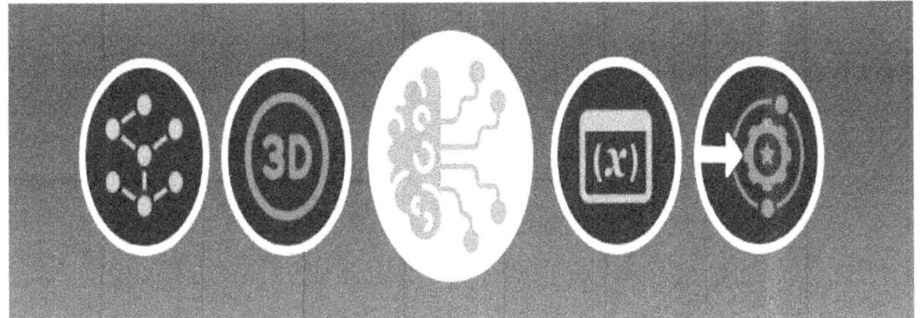

Fig 4.1: Generative AI Is Redefining Creative Innovation

4.2. Understanding Generative AI

Generative AI is defining the next chapter of how technology interacts with the world. There's more to a generative neural network than appearances. Rather, it can generate content for others to experience. This means that a generative neural network can create a wide range of content and solutions for a problem it is being trained on, such as music, speech, or novel style transfer. It's defining the future of technology through powerful neural networks that create photos of cats and people who do not exist, while others create entire music collections. Despite its abilities, there are situations where it does not work, like drawing a new picture of a cat without looking like a Picasso, simply because that's what the AI has been trained on.

A generative adversarial network model is a good example of generative AI: it exists in two parts, one that creates the content and another that determines if it is fake or not. Any type of generator is effectively an extension or variation of these abilities but adapted to operate on its respective object of focus as efficiently as existing algorithms do. Text generators generate a new sentence based on previous input in much the same way that style generators create new images based on contextual descriptions. These "contextual generators" can maintain style over multiple sentences or paragraphs, while conditional logic allows for more advanced control over the kind of images or sounds created. While systems like these are impressive, they nonetheless have trouble with consistency and can't generally understand or write full-blown scientific papers or novels.

Equation 1: AI Efficiency in Business Processes

$$E = f(T, R, A)$$

Where:

- T = Time saved due to AI automation

- R = Resource savings (e.g., human labor, computational resources)

- A = Accuracy improvement (reducing errors in tasks)

4.2.1. Definition and Basics

At its simplest, generative AI encompasses any computational system that produces genuinely new content. Within the framework of deep learning, such systems are most often based on large-scale neural network systems and training via machine learning methods. More effective still is unsupervised training, where genuinely novel content that is less reliant on derivative examples from human trainers may be coaxed from the systems. In many cases, generative AI requires a serious computational investment, whether through the direct energy costs of running the systems or indirectly through the human hours invested in programming, maintaining, and training the generative systems. The resulting systems nonetheless make that investment worthwhile. In their most advanced forms, systems trained to produce novel content can generate everything from complete drawings to photo-realistic people to novel scientific materials.

As a field, generative AI combines the little ooze of associative memories with the vast power of modern statistical models such as knowledge graphs and machine learning. In recent years, computer systems design has become dominated by deep learning, and within this approach, a very particular form of model, known as a neural network, dominates generative AI.

Advances in neural networks have been driven by the intersecting efforts of computational neuroscientists, computer scientists, and mathematicians. The first applications of neural networks emulated in shallow models the multiscale communications of the brain at the level of individual cells and, with them, the fluctuations among biochemical mediators. Like their biological counterparts, these models could only hunt for patterns in the data that were of a similar orthogonal or low degree, and hence they struggled to learn from the correlated patterns that data for most of human interest represents. In response, these early neural network models were rearranged. They turned out to be less competent than shallower, statistically based models whose constituent units or nodes were not modeled to communicate as closely as neurons, but the deeply arranged models demonstrated a vital feature that would come to define generative AI models: they could be trained.

4.2.2. Types of Generative AI

Generative AI models come in different flavors. Broadly speaking, today we can distinguish three major classes: text generators, image synthesizers, and sound creation tools. Each of these types has generated thousands of practical applications in a unique blend of artistic subfields and down-to-earth business processes. In the first type, generative AI models are trained to create text following the rules of fluent natural language. On the other extreme, we find generative music, where a computer uses knowledge about music theory to create sequences of sound. We find many tools and software intersecting both those extremes, such as visual generators that apply style transfer to images and create new works by blending visual textures, text-to image translation, and audio synthesis using text prompts.

Each of these types of generative AI can serve different business purposes beyond the purely creationist goals common in the field of AI-generated art. We can distinguish several applications in the areas of content and product creation, design, marketing, and business innovation. Text generators are often integrated with chatbots. Text and image generators are often used in content production and can be employed for the customer-facing side. Sound generators are often a neat feature for websites, rather than serious business technology. The field of generative AI is rapidly growing, and new refinements for these classes appear almost every year. Newer models outperform the original versions, and more nuanced divisions could be introduced to this taxonomy.

4.3. Applications in Business Processes

In recent years, generative artificial intelligence has been proposed as a transformative idea that can help businesses change their way of operating at the process level. One group of business processes that generate AI's capabilities in generating near-human-like artifacts using less time and labor are content generation tasks, such as music generation. Practices, including gaming, healthcare, and design, that are actively adopting generative AI solutions for supporting their creative practices, such as content making, are witnessing positive changes in productivity and experience.

Generative AI-enabled personalized marketing is a pervasive technique applied by many businesses in the service industry. It enables a company to customize the customer experience and connect the customer process workflows with their internal service workflows. For example, utilizing generative AI in professional resume generation creates customer pain points data in their workflow and informs them to be more creative in their services. Further, the services in CPG and FMCG industries, like customizing/packaging goods, can also benefit from the applications of generative AI for customization services, thus adding more business process offerings. However, it is worth noting that the potential transformation benefits will not come without concerns. Generative AI-enabled new business processes and the new revenue streams they can generate may create winner-takes-all effects in various forms of increasing returns that tend to favor a few large-scale platforms or companies and lead to changes in workforce dynamics, potential loss in consumer surplus, and privacy concerns.

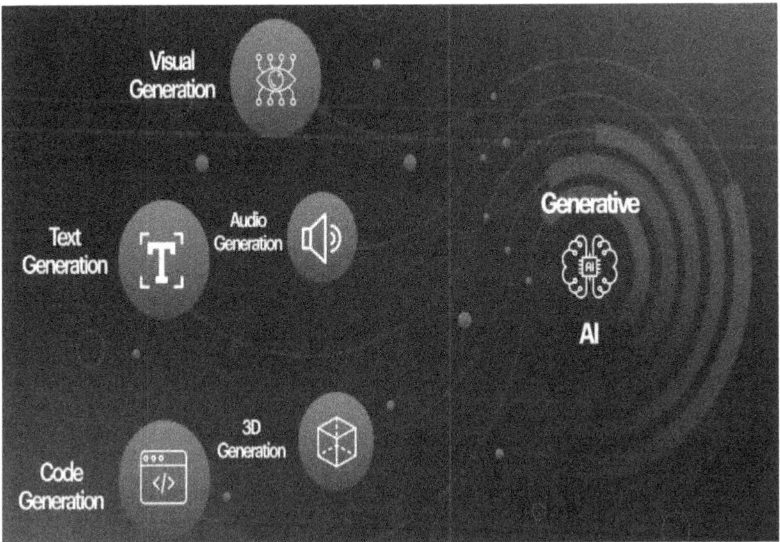

Fig 4.2: Generative AI Applications

4.3.1. Automated Content Generation

Automated content generation is integrated into various business processes. Several tools leverage generative AI, also known as creative AI, to assist in the production of written text, images, videos, and other content types. These AI-based tools can turn outlines into full-blown reports, generate unique titles for written material, translate audio into text and vice versa, make memes, produce artwork, and combine facial expressions with body language to create plausible character animations. These automated tools have the potential to be deployed by most businesses to drive up their output of external and internal material. By minimizing the amount of human involvement, both time and money can be saved. A substantial increase in minor social media updates means that human capital can be mobilized for other more important activities. It cites data showing that stories written and produced by this automated solution are on par with those generated by real people. It posits a situation where a journalist uses AI to write a story. The writer would have to maintain the right balance and timing, ensuring the AI does not get too creative, make mistakes, or take over the authorship. AI-generated stories would not be picked up by guest blogs since AI writers lack authenticity. AI stories would not be published at all in the first place if writers fail to provide the content creator with thorough instructions on how to produce insights. This shows the importance of balancing AI content and human oversight in content generation. A proposed split in favor of human oversight would give a solid infusion of brand voice, leaving room for AI inspiration and freeing up time for other creative tasks.

4.3.2. Personalized Marketing Strategies

One innovative approach of generative AI in the field of personalization can be observed in marketing strategies, offering a groundbreaking, innovative approach for tailor-made consumer engagement. While small businesses can obtain and process consumer preferences in real-time, collecting firsthand rich knowledge, companies, in general, collect readily available data on consumer behavior, promotions, and communication history, which is utilized for creating adjusted marketing tools. For example, a social network can use posts and messages to extract preferences, linking this information with data analytics for an automated advertisement posting tool. Several strategies create a personalized approach based on the data, such as:

- Targeted ad campaigns that make use of consumers' country, gender, age, activity, and social network users' expected number of clicks, paying only for clicks. - Product recommendation techniques that utilize the most up-to-date data on which users clicked which advertisement and bought which products, extracted from users' profiles, to present a list of the most suitable responses to a query. - Confirming purchase or selection since a template-based social network post-testing framework can be utilized for better detecting the desired product through analyzing behavioral data.

One expected result of personalized ads is an increase in customer loyalty and customer lifetime value. Generative AI, however, adds a level of complexity to marketing strategies. Marketers must tread cautiously regarding data collection and security to avoid revealing to customers that the company learns about them through eavesdropping, which resonates very badly in terms of trust if exposed in the media. In addition, these efforts should be handled very carefully regarding the legal aspects as they raise many ethical and legal concerns. Overall, though, personalized experiences are seen as herding audiences towards desired states with greater efficiency than generic mass marketing.

4.4. Impact on Creativity

Generative AI, as a key element of AI that provides tools for human innovation, is often considered one of the most transformative AI technologies. It builds on creative workflows that incorporate generative engines or systems that are uniquely enabled by AI. This means that, in practice, generative engines have been developed and applied in almost every creative field that involves the generation of original content, such as product design, web design, type design, filmmaking, photography, writing, and music.

Generative AI expands the possibilities of human work, freeing human artists, creators, and professionals from repetitive tasks and expanding their potential to innovate. It also leverages the cognitive biases found within data to generate original examples that are quantitatively self-similar or categorically self-similar. Many creative professionals have already adopted generative AI technologies for fundamental innovation within their field. Although it might sound crazy, in the digital age, there are more and more machines working in the creative process—either creating music, writing a novel, or cooking an outstanding culinary dish. Many generative AI novels, classical music compositions, and recipes now win internationally relevant prizes or recognition. Of course, human authors need to provide tags, themes, or seeds to generate AI. Meanwhile, some AI-generated novels are compared with the works of famous novelists. The AI version has won some challenges. Does that mean AI has become a novelist? Or how do we define a novelist's creativity and their works? This question still lies in one of AI's distinguished research fields, i.e., human-like and machine-like creativity.

Equation 2: AI and Creative Output in Business

$$C - h(Q, V, R, T)$$

Where:

- Q = Quality of creative output (e.g., design, content)

- V = Volume of output (amount of content generated)

- R = Resource utilization (how much AI reduces the need for human labor or computational cost)

- T = Time efficiency (the time taken to generate creative outputs)

4.4.1. Enhancing Creative Workflows

By making it easier to create, manage, and deliver insights from unstructured data, generative AI can help streamline creative workflows and optimize conceptualization efforts. GAI tools can help automate recurring contextual tasks. For instance, although GAI cannot replace a sketch artist or illustrator in its entirety, it could be used to generate the first draft after interpreting written requirements, providing an early sense of style and project experience. By doing this, the human illustrator's or designer's time is focused on conceptual ideation backed by concrete experiments, shortening the project duration. GAI can also serve as inspiration for "blockers" in creative workflows, such as writer's block, by creating unexpected plot swerves or graphical explorations.

In user interface and product design, it is becoming more common to perform several iterations via testing before launching a final product. Although ethics might raise concerns, leveraging GAI to auto generate UX/UI prototypes increases the number of initial alternatives to test and democratizes design since data-based decisions are more representative of the target audience's preferences. In literature, GAI can suggest drafts when a creator struggles or needs new ideas. Additionally, GAI can also generate layout alternatives, harmony, and compositional rules for paintings and other conceptual art. That is, GAI serves as an idea promoter and endpoint validator.

4.4.2. Collaboration between AI and Human Creativity

An alternative approach to considering AI's relationship with human artistic creativity does not view the activities of each in purely adversarial terms, where the AI is a threat to creativity and creative livelihood, but as a potential collaborator in the creative enterprise. While they have attempted to cast aside the AI system's model for generating designs, artists have found uses for the underlying AI systems in their work, arguing that the systems serve better not as creative "assistants" but more as exteriorizations of certain parts of their creative processes. That might sound simply like an evolution of the role of artists' tools in digital media, computers, and digital software, but these artists frame their incorporation of AI models as part of the exploration of their creative processes. They are not simply adding new tools to their kit that allow them to put high quantities of work out into the world, but exploring what depth of value exists in a different model of creativity altogether.

This idea of generative AI is having its greatest impact on industries where creativity is in high demand and low supply, or where creativity is essential to the field. One large field influenced is music, with the most successful applications of the technology so far appearing in music. Starting in 2016, researchers and companies began to leverage generative AI in music, in the creation of music for everything from commercials to soundtracks, and in what could be understood as the first major money contest in AI music. While AI music digital goods have been met with some skepticism, others have found new ways to incorporate other people's AI into their creative work. As in the visual arts, how individual musicians interact with these collaborations is varied and showcases just how creative our imitation can be. What we might be moving towards is a new model where creativity is related to what we make. And will the role of AI and creativity come to be understood in a way that is governed not by the loss of creativity or creative jobs, but by the creation of new data, new work, and new experiences?

4.5. Challenges and Ethical Considerations

Many of these technologies also hold the promise to seamlessly augment human creativity, but they also raise unique challenges. To bring AI models that are both creative and empathetic to the real world requires not only sophisticated benchmarks and training methodologies but interdisciplinary training frameworks and partnerships based upon social sciences, philosophy of mind, and cognitive sciences, as well as the creation of technological tools that foster best practices for responsible AI research that are available to everyone. Additionally, the effects of generative models on the real world and creativity are profoundly influenced by culture and social practices. Ethical and legal frameworks on intelligent systems are complex and can be informed by ethical principles relevant to humans, but they must be tailored to the unique concerns that arise when AI falls outside the legal and ethical frameworks of existing technologies.

Moreover, policy and compliance experts agree that companies will be held to account if they deploy systems acting on the cutting edge of what is technologically possible and politically acceptable. These criticisms can contribute to a continuing slow adoption of AI and data technologies in several sectors and could even lead to overly restrictive data-related laws. In this text, we aim to discuss how to utilize generative AI to build models that do more than create artificial images that are patently fake, how AI-driven creativity and innovation could affect the world of business, how it can lead to growth and efficiency, and how it might change to redefine certain industrial sectors.

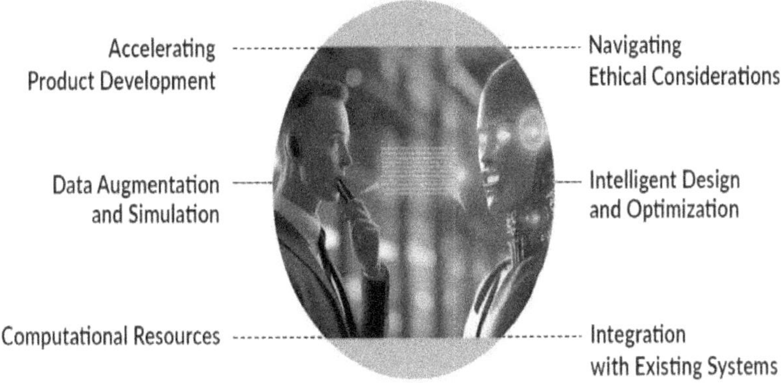

Fig 4.3: Challenges Do Generative AI Solutions Solve for Businesses

4.6. Conclusion

Generative AI technologies are revolutionizing businesses by changing processes and increasing creativity in teams. This survey introduced generative AI and summarized a number of the advancements before turning to recent developments both inside and outside of enterprises. The essay outlined some of the potential benefits as well as some of the socio-technological disruptions and limitations associated with incorporating these new AI capabilities into organizational procedures. We also raised ethical questions, especially concerning the training data used to develop these models, before concluding with the anticipation of several potential future applications. In conclusion, generative AI technologies have a significant role to play in redefining organizational processes and creativity in the workplace. There are benefits to be gained from using the technology if used appropriately. These might be enhanced as new functionalities arise, as the limitations of these tools decrease, and as research addresses concerns raised in this survey issue. However, if organizations fail to adapt to the trends and the potential technological advancements mentioned, they will likely fall behind. Organizations must keep abreast of the advancements in the transfer of recent AI research into systems and services for corporate use if they are to remain competitive, particularly against new entrants to the IT services sector.

Equation 3: AI's Influence on Customer Experience

$$CX - j(P, A, T, C)$$

Where:

- P = Personalization (how AI tailors experiences to individual customers)

- A = Automation (automation of customer service, recommendations, etc.)

- T = Time (faster response times, instant customer support)

- C = Consistency (maintaining a consistent customer experience across touchpoints)

4.6.1. Future Trends

In the future, the flattening of the barriers to entry of generative AI systems through low-code interfaces will enable small and medium enterprises, larger corporations, and AI start-ups to build reimagined solutions to unlock more value from data and then operationalize those AI innovations into the core of the business. Within five years, it is believed that start-up founders, entrepreneurs, and business leaders will not only use these reimagined solutions from others but build these solutions themselves to stay competitive and innovative in the industries they operate within. Future trends will also involve more personalization of content and creativity for end users, and the broader trend of 'AI everywhere' meaning the AI layer will not be something software engineers think about separately, but rather a component they integrate into the everyday tools they already use.

The impacts of these future trends will be widespread, with virtually every industry affected - and a particular focus on the ad tech, marketing, and e-commerce sectors. Significant opportunities to leverage these future trends specifically exist in improving productivity for sales and marketing professionals through an AI inside approach that automates tasks and procedural creativity. As such, this infrastructure will sit alongside closely related technologies reimagining the ways businesses generate insights from data or coordinate software and systems based on those insights. It is expected that businesses will face a range of challenges in implementing AI capabilities, including governance and privacy, with a growing focus on consensus for ethical principles, regulatory oversight, and a shift from formal training of large-scale AI models to widening the focus from training to deployment, adoption, and usage. As such, businesses and individuals alike have to be prepared to adapt to a rapidly changing environment, with new roles, skills, and operating models required. Additionally, it is expected that regulators will be trying to find more ways to restrict the reach and possibility of ethical harm from AI.

References

[1]Liu, B., & Zhang, Y. (2021). The role of big data and AI in reshaping the organizational landscape. Business Horizons, 64(5), 689-698. https://doi.org/10.1016/j.bushor.2021.05.004

[2]Ma, H., & Wang, S. (2020). Generative AI and big data: Transforming organizational efficiency and scalability. Journal of Technology Management & Innovation, 15(2), 107-122.

[3]Marr, B. (2019). The big data analytics revolution: Data-driven strategies for organizational success. Wiley.

[4]McKinsey & Company. (2020). The state of AI in 2020: Accelerating business transformation through AI and big data. McKinsey Global Institute.

[5]Mehta, S., & Patel, R. (2021). Harnessing generative AI for business innovation. Journal of AI Research and Development, 5(3), 123-140. https://doi.org/10.1016/j.jair.2020.12.009

5

Data-Driven Innovation: Fostering Organizational Agility and Competitiveness

5.1. Introduction

In today's rapidly changing market, both individuals and organizations must continuously orient towards data-driven strategies in order to survive and maintain their competitive edge. Consequently, it becomes crucial for both support functions and senior management within organizations to understand how to foster technological and business capabilities, with the aim of achieving agility and competitiveness. While support functions require these capabilities in order to develop and implement innovative tools and methodologies to support decisions, the digital transformation requires a new strategic class of senior management, fostering the development of data-driven innovation and organizational agility to guarantee their competitiveness. In fact, it is well known that adaptive management has become a necessity. Organizations are today operating in an ecosystem characterized by radical and unpredictable change. Managers have to make decisions without knowing with certainty what tomorrow will bring. Moreover, we are currently experiencing an explosion of data. It has been highlighted that within the last few years, more data have been produced than during the entire previous history, and it is expected that in 2025 alone there will be an estimated 463 exabytes of data each day across the globe, a 10× increase from 2022.

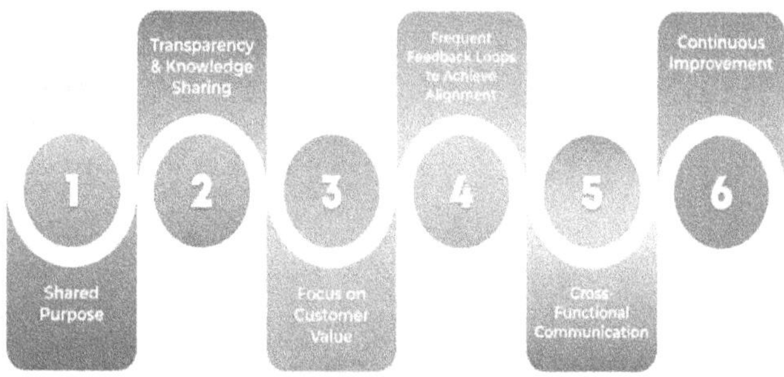

Fig 5.1: Organizational Agility

5.1.1. Background and Rationale

By identifying changes in worker efficiency and data-related organizational tasks, we show that within the data-driven innovation domain, organizational activity is seeing the benefits of efficiency-enhancing competitive incentives. By explaining the natural payoff, a multifaceted link between data-driven decision-making and organizational agility has been replicated. Scholars also highlight the advantages of data-driven decision-making expertise, particularly its potential to make businesses more flexible. It is impossible to iterate on innovation without knowledge of the organization's purpose. Still, researchers tend to largely dominate the conversation on organizational agility. Scholars tend to concentrate on the function and methods of the potential data-driven decision-making - the competitiveness spotlight. We are aiming to see information technology through the prism of industry and competitiveness. By developing a bigger context, we bridge the methodological gap between earlier technology acceptance research and our enablers. Our predictive approach is not bound but is indeed widely based on existing work in order to provide organizational accomplishments that are context-dependent. Although data-driven practices have more extensive practical implications, an understanding of the data-driven decision-making benefits will help build organizational contingencies and policies within organizations already pursuing these strategic options. For both scholars and innovators, we argue that it is useful to know theoretically. Conversely, for use in practical terms, a greater understanding of data-driven decision-making can be used to respond to organizational agility at the immediate operational level. Identifying organizational data-driven decision-making variables will support strategic researchers and leaders throughout the industry in discovering common points of view and dynamic competitive solutions emerging from them.

5.1.2. Research Aim and Objectives

The primary aim of this research study is to investigate the relationship between "Data-Driven Innovation and Organizational Agility" and the ongoing digital and business transformation, focusing on how organizations can leverage data insights to foster a culture of continuous innovation and competitiveness. Software firms and software product development are the primary fields of this study. However, the research findings could be used as good practice by other industries. The study aims to achieve the following objectives. It also highlights the key drivers of successful data innovation implementation. - Objective 1: To explore the implications of data-driven innovation on software development processes. - Objective 2: To scrutinize the four data-driven enablers and antecedents—competition, data resources, IT infrastructure, and strategic importance—from a practitioner's lens. - Objective 3: To investigate how strategic and operational ambidextrous practices affect idiosyncratic data-driven innovation in software firms. Objective 4: To identify the challenges of data implementation from a non-data company's perspective. - How do software organizations perceive and use data-driven innovation to affect their software development processes in general and performance.

5.2. Understanding Data-Driven Innovation

Data-driven innovation is achieved when organizations find unique ways to drive value from data, which could be customer, operational, informational, or emerging data, by generating data-driven products, creating new data-driven services or markets, or driving current efficiencies via data-driven methods. This broad definition encompasses a wide range of innovation activity, from how organizations use data to drive new technologies, products, or services in a dedicated innovation and experimentation unit, to how an organization integrates data collection, processing, and use as part of 'business as usual.' Nurturing data-driven innovation initiatives helps organizations develop new value from the data they receive or collect, helping an organization to gain a data-driven competitive advantage, adapt to change, differentiate themselves from competitors, grow, and expand. Data-driven innovation is developing the use of big data and analytics to generate novel solutions to operational issues, including in-house organizational innovations, market-led innovations, and those not seen directly as an innovation strategy.

Innovation is 'the introduction of a new (or significantly improved) good or service that has found some degree of success in the time of study.' The data used in the innovation must be seen as decisive and influential, being a key tool for the creation of new services and products. Data has the potential to overcome these process bottlenecks by competing with the previous best practices and previously unknown creative solutions. This understanding highlights that innovation through data processes could reflect a type of apparent evolutionary process, even if the process itself reports are not related to the procedure of the innovation process of the organization.

Equation 1: Innovation Performance (IP) Equation

$$IP - f(D, C, A, T)$$

Where:

- D = **Data Quality** (e.g., accuracy, completeness, timeliness of data)

- C = **Collaboration** (degree of collaboration between teams, departments, or external partners in using data for innovation)

- A = **Analytics Capability** (organization's ability to analyze and interpret data for actionable insights)

- T = **Technology Infrastructure** (availability of the right tools and platforms for storing, processing, and analyzing data)

5.2.1. Definition and Concepts

Innovation, in general, is the process by which enterprises convert knowledge into new or significantly improved products, services, or processes. Data-driven innovation involves the use and exploitation of data to inform decisions and optimize the design of innovations, and to help predict and monitor product performance for warranty and performance management. Accordingly, knowledge discovery and insight, usually described as analytics, attained from the data collected and generated within and external to the enterprise, is a significant part of data-driven innovation. This can occur throughout the life of the innovation, including not just idea generation and knowledge during the design and manufacturing process, but also analytics of products in the field post-manufacture. Data-driven innovation may also involve the innovation of the business process underpinning the product or service, or the discovery of new business strategies in the context of new markets, thus improving the innovation management process.

Data-driven innovation is not a totally new concept in the innovation literature, but it has gained prominent attention in this era of digitization, big data, IoT, and advanced manufacturing, among others. The literature underlines that the use of data, often referred to as big data, in business is multidimensional. For instance, data that are used can be internal or external; it can be used analytically and also in the form of big data. Moreover, it can be used in isolation as well as in combination with other sources of data. The operative use of data in the innovation process of organizations is embodied by the term data-driven innovation, which essentially signifies a major break from the traditional approach to acquiring and processing information. Data-driven innovation, as a strategic management practice, differs from operational transaction processing in the sense that the purpose and consumer of the output of the information system are of a different nature.

5.2.2. Benefits and Challenges

Nevertheless, attracting competitive advantages in the modern data-innovation environment is not easy, as it comes with different challenges. These challenges include the limitations of today's big data tools and methods; the expertise and skills that data-related scientific and IT staff need to develop actionable data innovation; hoarding and extracting value from the data; and concerns about data privacy. Some people think that getting access to endless data and computing power is enough to take advantage of the value of data innovation, which is not the case. Data-oriented leaders have pushed their organizations towards a steadier commitment to moving to a data-driven strategy. However, observing these barriers and turning them into opportunities is crucial to making the move toward data-driven innovation a more value-creating endeavor. In recent years, non-automated big data tools have moved towards a focus on action, data insights, and direct revenue creation. Nonetheless, it is vital to be aware of the current situation in today's industrial developments. The challenge of data insight creation and processing from a methodological point of view is very challenging. These challenges primarily refer to methodological issues related to imperfect data, systems directives, and organization-dependent factors.

5.3. Organizational Agility and Competitiveness

In increasingly digitally oriented marketplaces characterized by rapid change and ambiguity, organizational agility has become a key concern for corporate strategists and leadership. Conceptually, organizational agility is argued to manifest in improved time to market, lower costs, and higher quality of products, services, and digital activities. There is much to be learned about how organizational agility is translated into competitive advantage. Given the formidable rate of change and increasing disruptive potential encountered in digital transformation, it is incumbent on leadership to better coordinate this asset set in creating organizations that are responsive to change. This critical link in terms of research on organizational agility is essential: that is, what does organizational agility mean in the context of competitiveness, a principal research agenda for digital transformation, and a potential source of competitive advantage itself?

5.3.1. Conceptual Framework

Organizational agility can only be realized if people who make decisions are able to use data from data warehouses and business intelligence tools in the decision-making processes. Thus, using a large set of data within the organization can pave the way for innovation. Innovation is driven by the strategic intent of senior managers to create a technology-enabled game changer. Data-driven innovation can take place by changing the performance or functionality of a product or process, changing the user experience, creating a new context in which customers or partners can use existing products or services, and changing the ecosystem in which products or services interact with others. There is a rich practice and research suggesting a handful of approaches towards achieving innovation. These include but are not limited to, management of technology, resource-based view, open innovation, as well as the practice based on build-measure-learn.Organizational agility hinges on the ability of decision-makers to leverage data from data warehouses and business intelligence tools, enabling informed, strategic decisions that foster innovation. By integrating vast amounts of data into the decision-making process, organizations can unlock new avenues for creativity and advancement. Innovation, in this context, is often propelled by the strategic vision of senior leaders who embrace technology as a catalyst for transformative change. This can manifest in various forms, such as enhancing the functionality of products or processes, improving user experiences, creating novel contexts for existing products or services, or reshaping ecosystems where these products or services interact.

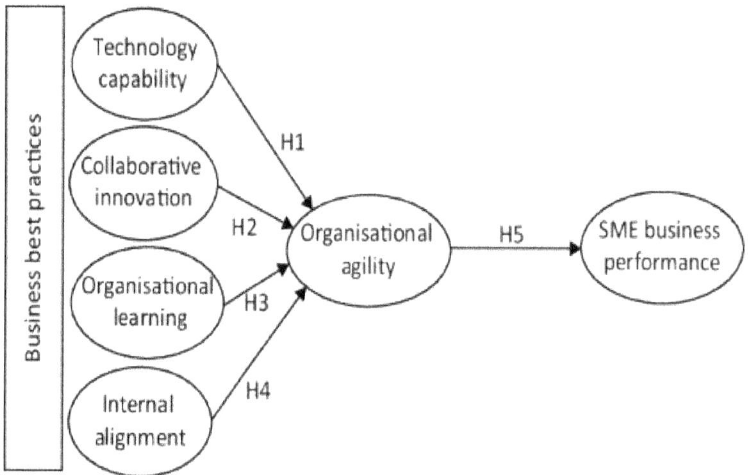

Fig 5.2: Conceptual framework for organisational agility

5.3.2. The Role of Data-Driven Innovation

In the context of rapid changes in society and markets, agility is increasingly recognized as a key driver of organizational competitiveness and resilience. From a digital perspective, data is at the heart of current corporate transformation. Yet, how exactly do insights extracted from data affect operational effectiveness? The most direct and widely recognized impact of being data-driven is the improvement in understanding what customers need and want, in making strategic decisions that stay ahead of the competition, and in launching new customer products and services. However, cases of data-driven organizations are still quite uncommon.

Technology can be an additional and enabling pathway to agility. The role of IT infrastructure can be complemented with adequate software solutions. Data-driven innovation enables organizations to anticipate the future and react rapidly by identifying new data sources, experimenting with new business models, and having a thoroughly data-driven decision-making process entrenching all levels of their organization. However, this analysis is a bit shallow since, first, being data-driven is a difficult challenge for any organization, and, second, data management strategic aspects remain mostly unaddressed, especially data utilization and the role of data governance in BI scalability.

5.4. Case Studies and Examples

To supplement our survey data on the state of data-driven innovation and strategy in the enterprise, we present several real-world case studies. These illustrate how data strategies have been implemented (or have failed to be implemented) in practice and have led to quantifiable improvements in agility and competitiveness. Organizations and industries represented in our case studies are diverse, including software, manufacturing, large data center operations, public consulting, marketing, sporting events, and consumer technologies. An analysis of our cases offers several identifiable common themes: 1. Fostering a strong data culture is critical. 2. Success requires goal setting. 3. Standardizing on modern tools speeds progress. 4. Being outlier-focused drives economies of scale. What can other organizations learn from our case studies? Many factors can ease the creation of a data-driven organization, including a willingness to take risks, investment in modern tools, and an openness to learning from and meaningfully addressing mistakes. Interestingly, the organizations themselves were all medium or large in size and had multi-year experience in the space, but their level of success in gaining the benefits of data innovation varied greatly. A majority of organizations adopting data innovation strategies report at least some benefit; only a fraction of these firms report specific and significant business improvements. The business gains of committed analytics users are large compared to those of firms that either have no analytical success or are reporting only general business benefits.

Equation 2: Organizational Agility (OA) Equation

$$OA - \frac{S}{R}$$

Where:

- S = Speed of Data Utilization (how fast the organization can gather, analyze, and act on data insights)

- R = Resistance to Change (organizational inertia, including culture, structure, and processes that slow adaptation to data-driven decisions)

5.4.1. Successful Implementation Stories

Implementing a business intelligence solution is by no means an easy task for any organization. However, the task of getting to know their clients better and the desire to better assess employee performance comes particularly easy to organizations in a service-oriented business. The collected stories acknowledge the complexity of customer data, particularly in businesses where dividing the essential data from the nonessential is by no means intuitive, nor is it an easy task. However, in both these cases, organizations were successful in harnessing the power of data and strategically implementing it to drive their business. A major challenge for most of these stories was the considerable effort expended in getting infrastructure into place, including the automation of data collection processes.

Success stories such as these provide us with crucial insights. The stories in this section present real-world vignettes based on organizations that have started using data to help them in decision-making. We hope these stories will serve as inspiration and potentially useful case studies for other organizations considering starting to use data or changing data strategy. The stories are presented in two separate sub-sections, according to the resulting case studies. Success stories are organized into two larger sub-sections, each describing an organization or business function that has successfully utilized data. Each contains a collection of best efforts able to give some lessons on best implementation. In sum, the success stories in this section are published as ten separate collections. Each is organized according to the sub-section to which it belongs. Each story may be read individually or all together in a subsequent section.

5.4.2. Lessons Learned

- Not having a clear strategy of how to use data and analytics may be one obstacle. Yet another issue is that employees still find it hard to understand how analytics initiatives are going to pan out and to see the benefits. This can be addressed by: 1) establishing a data strategy before dealing with a data analytics initiative; 2) training employees regularly on data and analytics; and 3) investing in a collaborative culture within the organization. - Providing valuable insights means nothing if some technical issues impede them from being turned into actual benefits. This makes top-down initiatives more efficient than those of individual business units unless data science has already been experienced in the organization, in which case a mix of the two is the most efficient technique. Leveraging data and analytics as seamlessly as possible into existing business processes is the most effective way to turn inputs of data analytics into business outputs that will help lead the organization forward. Indeed, outputs from an analytics initiative can be both inputs for other analytics phases or directly serve as inputs for specific, useful products for the organization. Ultimately, the better and more securely stored the data, the more potential outputs from analytics projects for current and future utilities.

5.5. Conclusion and Future Directions

This paper has contributed to the literature by suggesting that data-driven innovation is an agility emerging within organizations, and one that allows them to use data-driven insights reactively and proactively to become more efficient, foster more agility, and deliver new services. We have used five relevant case studies of varying complexities and have shown that they benefited in different ways from data-driven innovations. Therefore, practically, as the cost and footprint of technology reduce, data-driven innovation is becoming viable and scalable for any organization with respect to their size and capabilities for occurring disruptions independently from their source. Our research outputs implore future studies in this domain and practice in this domain of digital disruptions and leveraging the value of data-driven innovations in an organizational context. We conclude by noting that organizations that make a serious effort towards developing and adopting a data-driven approach in pursuit of innovation will be viewed more favorably than those that do not. This is in aid of the enhanced agility that stems from the accumulation of evidence and insights to reveal opportunities and threats, make better decisions, and predict the needs of stakeholders and potential customers. For this reason, enterprises can no longer afford to fail to take advantage of these opportunities, even in the shadow of potential disruptions.

5.5.1. Key Findings and Implications

Our research has a number of implications. First, it explicitly shows that those organizations willing and able to use data effectively to drive innovation and inform decision-making are demonstrably more agile. Second, flexibility and open-mindedness on the part of an organization are key. Third, it reveals that leaders who do not actually use data are at a distinct disadvantage because they are less adaptable and have poorer decision-making processes. Given that data-driven innovation and agility result in various forms of competitive advantage, they necessitate transformational change to effectively support adaptation.

The need for data-driven innovation and agility also results in barriers that professionals will face when trying to achieve such an ambitious organizational shift. We focus on data quality, silos on data and/or in organizations, and the promotion of numbers as a 'truth' with pre-thought embedded into visualization. To overcome these barriers, we find that approaches need to move away from top-down change to reflective and responsible adoption of data practices. Data professionals need to be given space for creative implementation at ground roots, time to negotiate institutional culture and effect broad-based shifts before giving full accountability of data practices to an individual at the top, or a 'data' leader or CDO.

Equation 2: Competitive Advantage (CA) Equation

$$CA - \frac{D_i \times T_r}{C_c \times I}$$

Where:

- D_i = **Data Insights** (unique, actionable insights derived from data analysis)

- T_r = **Technology Resilience** (ability of the technology infrastructure to adapt, scale, and integrate emerging technologies)

- C_c = **Competitor Data Capability** (the data capabilities and analytics strength of competitors)

- I = **Internal Innovation Capability** (capacity to innovate within the organization based on data insights)

5.5.2. Future Trends

Technological advancements are one of the main drivers of future innovation. Artificial intelligence is already accelerated by machine learning algorithms on large-scale data and self-evolving cloud computing capabilities, and it is expected to rise significantly. In this scenario, multi-destination challenges corporate innovators themselves, even when positioned in technology-driven companies, because some major ingredients that contribute to the market have been traditionally neglected by innovation strategy, including design and market capabilities. The predictions on the future of technology-related innovation show that evolving data analytics will enhance organizational agility. More powerful technologies are changing corporate behavior to act in response to advanced data results. A reactive new dimension of planned data-driven innovation could be supported by arguing that current enterprise practices should suit the competitive future scenario. This is why organizations should actively start to design managerial capabilities to integrate a growing level of data into corporate strategy now.

References

[1]Mishra, P., & Joshi, M. (2022). Big data-driven decision making in modern businesses. Business Analytics Journal, 30(4), 145-158. https://doi.org/10.1007/s10370-022-00895-0 [2]Möller, K., & Rajala, A. (2017). Organizational transformation through big data analytics. Journal of Strategic Marketing, 25(3), 201-218. https://doi.org/10.1080/0965254X.2016.1244660 [3]O'Reilly, T., & Sasson, S. (2018). WTF: What's the future and why it's up to us. Harper Business. [4]Peltier, S., & Guo, Z. (2020). The ethical implications of AI and big data in business. Journal of Business Ethics, 162(3), 553-568. https://doi.org/10.1007/s10551-019-04337-0 [5]PwC. (2021). AI and big data in business: New possibilities for scalability and growth. PricewaterhouseCoopers.

6

Big Data and Generative AI in Enhancing Customer Experience

6.1. Introduction

Technological advances have today transformed the way that consumers interact. When a generation ago interacting with a business meant being greeted by a shop owner who knew the regulars by name, now scores of companies each year interact with customers through their screens. Businesses whose success once depended upon personalized service behind their products now serve entire populations in a completely virtual manner. Motivated by the volumes of data that could be acquired through digital interfaces, these businesses now conceive of their customers not as people defined by preferences and personality but as segments in equations designed to represent probability and risk. This essay will demonstrate that by employing a data science strategy, customer service can, and is in fact in the process of taking on a completely new form. It will show that big data and generative AIs will transform customer service and also how they carry potential pitfalls that might hold back large-scale change to the customer experience.

Fig 6.1: Generative AI in Customer Experience

6.1.1. Background and Significance

Big data analytics has received increasing attention because of the competitive advantage that early adopters of the technology can gain. Not only must firms collect and store consumer data in a structured and easily accessible manner, but they must also be able to employ algorithms for analyzing the data to generate a true competitive advantage. The insights drawn from big data that drive the development and execution of firm strategies can have a positive impact on long-term survival. Further, many organizations understand and believe that big data and data analytics in decision-making is a powerful tools that can drive efficiency and customer satisfaction. With more businesses investing resources to have a data analytics aspect of their firm, potential data scientists can thrive in a field that gives them a competitive advantage over others.

An additional benefit of big data has stemmed from generative artificial intelligence that is being employed to synthesize massive amounts of natural language data. By inputting a request or even providing a set of parameters into a generative AI, it can provide an output of synthetic human speech, connect emotional and empathetic outlooks based on context, compose poetry, or create vast datasets that can be used in an ever-expanding selection of fields.

6.1.2. Research Objectives

The main objective of this study is to dive deep into the world of big data and generative AI and investigate how they can be employed to take customer experience to a whole new level. Several specific research objectives are underlined, namely: • To conduct an in-depth literature review to understand the premises of big data, AI, generative AI, customer service, and the role of the human touch in business-customer relationships. • To investigate real-world applications of big data and/or generative AI in delivering unforgettable customer experiences. • To discuss the main intersections and differences between delivering a customer experience with generative AI versus with big data. • To investigate whether businesses currently adopting big data in their customer experience strategy are also currently implementing generative AI or are considering the possibility of doing so. • To identify the main obstacles encountered by organizations when implementing big data or AI technologies in their approach to creating unforgettable experiences for their clients. • To identify what companies wish for when it comes to the further development of customer-related technologies that they use or wish to use in the future. We wish to understand and reflect upon the requirements needed for the introduction of new technologies, but also their limits and the inequalities and risks they face or raise.

6.2. Understanding Big Data and Generative AI

Big data refers to datasets that are too large or complex to analyze with regular data management tools. They are characterized by the "3Vs," or the following: volume, velocity, and variety. Because of this, managing and analyzing big data is difficult. The term has since grown to encompass a wider number of characteristics, such as credibility, ethics, and the management of data. Generative AI refers to algorithms capable of producing content or automating processes, such as chatbots. When used properly, a percentage of companies report that generative AI can reduce customer service costs significantly. Big data is composed of structured data, which can be handled by machines, and unstructured data, which is qualitative, subjective, and often collected in the form of customer feedback, such as surveys or social media interaction. Big data and generative AI are typically used together to process and analyze customer data in order to optimize customer experiences. In addition to providing data, AI models can be used to automate data analysis, generating operations with customer intent as their focus. One application is the personalization of offers—a tactic implemented before and after the customer interaction. For example, service advisors may use a predictive analytics model to make financial product offers based on a customer's credit rating and transaction history. Additionally, companies can deploy chatbots to conduct these interactions and offer relevant products or services.

Equation 1: Customer Experience Enhancement Model (CXE)

$$CXE = f(BigData, GenerativeAI)$$

Where:

- CXE = Customer Experience Enhancement

- f = A function that models the impact of Big Data and Generative AI on customer experience. This could involve variables such as personalization, satisfaction, engagement, and response time.

6.2.1. Definitions and Concepts

The technical connotation of machine learning is that it is a data analysis method that automates the inference of complex patterns behind data, the creation of models, and the prediction of results from examples. Deep learning emphasizes the learning mechanism of model parameters through a deep neural network composed of multiple layers and nodes. In practical applications, entities can use generative AI to create landscapes, portrait sketches, videos, and other visuals for artistic production. A major function of generative AI is to generate long article content, a.k.a. text generation. Given a prompt, it uses the model to complete the passage. In terms of upscaling, generative AI creates visually appealing images, upscales heavily pixelated photos to more natural-looking high-resolution images, produces symbol-based faces and sketches, and transforms holiday photos into landscape masterpieces. Overall, generative AI refers to technology that synthesizes objects and creates content in natural form. This tech can be used for deep fake videos, content creation, visual art, and article authoring.

A major advantage of big data is not in the data but in the analytics, i.e., performing analytics on a larger volume of data to increase confidence in insights derived from the data. The increase in digital data handling has led to businesses intensifying their efforts to integrate more advanced approaches to maximizing their effectiveness and efficiency in big data. To that end, many organizations have introduced AI and its offshoot technologies such as big data analytics, machine learning, and generative AI. Techniques from the field have been solidified into methodologies and solutions that are readily accessible for business adoption and deployment.

6.2.2. Applications in Customer Experience Enhancement

Applications for Enhancing CX: Customer experience personalization through offering tailored and individual products, specialized services, or targeted marketing can lead to higher satisfaction and loyalty. Big data analytics is applied to identify long-term patterns and trends in customer behavior; therefore, appropriate reactions include new product launches, extended services, or a particular way to approach prospective customers with greater market acceptance. AI help desks and chatbots equipped with machine learning algorithms are increasingly in use within customer-driven industries to provide 24/7 service center assistance. As an AI-driven traditional service center, chatbots provide a faster and more convenient alternative for first-line customer service that can address simple and frequently asked questions. This results in a potential reduction in call volume, allowing human employees to concentrate on complex and less common cases. Predictive analytics anticipates what each customer is likely to do in their unique situation as identified by AI-driven algorithms. Financial services is one of the first and most popular industries to win the CX market by deploying predictive analytics solutions. Real-time communication improved the level of satisfaction in real-time.

6.3. Theoretical Framework

The theoretical framework underpins the study of the interconnectedness of Big Data and Generative AI in the context of customer experience related to applications between consumers and computers/technology. The study linked with the market comes from the viewpoint of Customer Experience Theory, the main role of Technological Determinism, Stewarding Theory, and Big Data Theory. Big Data has become an important issue in business and policy studies, one that straddles both social and physical science literature and thus has the capacity to connect many theoretical lenses to practical applications.

Diffusion of Innovations is a theory about how, why, and at what rate new ideas and technology spread. Generative AI's touchpoints with AI are used in the study, whose main underpinning theories include Technological Determinism and Turing's imitation game. These touchpoints represent the 'black box' aspects of AI that simulate human interactions, embodied by search engines, human-like robots that can complete tasks, voice recognition devices, and applications. The theoretical framework guiding the study of the interplay between Big Data and Generative AI in shaping customer experience revolves around several interconnected theories. Customer Experience Theory provides a lens to explore how consumers interact with technology, focusing on the emotional, cognitive, and sensory aspects of these engagements. Technological Determinism emphasizes the influence of technology in shaping human behavior and societal structures, suggesting that the evolution of Generative AI and Big Data fundamentally transforms consumer experiences. Stewarding Theory offers a perspective on the responsibility of businesses and organizations to manage and utilize these technologies ethically.

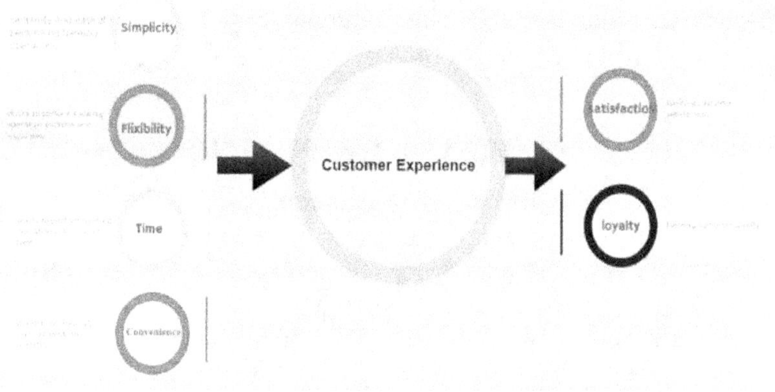

Fig 6.2: The theoretical framework for customer experience improvement

6.3.1. Customer Experience Theory

In a typical article, one can regularly find references to the benefits big data and, more specifically, generative AI can provide in our ability to tap into the mindset of today's modern consumer. Before we dive into such topics, a basic understanding of customer experience theory provides a good foundational basis to comprehend why tools that provide such insight are becoming necessities in the business world. At its core, customer experience theory sets out to determine that a customer is not fully satisfied until his or her personal feelings match ideally with the performance of the product or service. Today, we know this as customer satisfaction. However, the integration of the concepts of customer satisfaction with the emotional connections a customer has to product experiences is essential.

Taken more generally, this entire body of literature and opinion allows us to address what customer experience theory tells us. Specifically, current niche marketing strategies and product growth innovation marketing programs by their very nature address a general...

6.3.2. Big Data Theory

There are several different techniques and theories for big data processing and analysis. Data analytics demonstrate which types of analytical and learning methods and tactical tools could be applied to big data processing. Several tools and techniques to decipher and process big data are available. You can use the structured data that is stored in relational data storage either in how or XML structure to assist in tracking, measuring, retrieving, or storing data. The unstructured data also requires a structured dictionary or rule that efficiently stores big data either on the web or in a cloud computing database. Regression analysis is a statistical approach to study the primary relationship between a dependent variable and one or more independent variables. In big data, market entry highlights real challenges when taking advantage of big data, as necessary ethics and policies for the protection of personal data require respect. Companies have also developed fascinating techniques to analyze the operational enhancements introduced by big data. Predictive analytics has become essential recently. It is mainly fueled by big data, including digital data from various touch points along the consumer journey. With big data coming from even more consumer touchpoints, the potential for predictive analytics is rising. Companies must invest as well in determining which particular marks contribute to satisfaction and which actually do not. Big volumes of big data can be captured and utilized in order to understand new consumer segments better and forecast upcoming potentials. Strategy alignment within the business with big data results means managers that proactively have to harness big data outcomes and make strategic decisions based on them. The theory can be integrated into website strategy as follows: recognize new consumer groups; attract more visitors and possible buyers; and increase consumer satisfaction by targeting crucial consumer requirements.

6.3.3. Generative AI Theory

Generative AI refers to creating systems capable of generating content. Content can be from any domain, including text, images, audio, and video. Machine learning models like neural networks play a significant role in building generative AI systems. The primary algorithms used inside the neural networks for sequential data generation are called Recurrent Neural Networks, Long Short-Term Memory, and Transformer. For other data like images and audio, Convolutional Neural Networks are used. The advancement in generative AI technology has seen content that is indiscernible from human-generated content.

Interactions between humans and AI-generated output might place consumers in a slightly uncomfortable situation, particularly if they are conscious that the recommendation or response given to them by the AI chatbot is also probably being suggested to many other people. Some believe that too much usage of AI language systems could result in a loss of trust in the validity and authenticity of the content. These concerns spur more questions about who the final author of a piece of AI generation is: the machine or the human. Recognition that AI models are learning from human content has sounded the alarm bells of ethical considerations inside organizations for some time. Skills in providing data labeling to influence the dataset and, in turn, being able to somewhat steer an AI response might address this issue.

6.4. Methodology

Second to this, it is critical to incorporate primary data collection. While there are limitations to reliance on semi-structured data in such research, as interviews may possess constraints on freedom of response, it remains clear that these are integral in exploring socio-cultural implications present at an idiographic and interpretative level. These research tools were supported by an appreciable theoretical background to offer true understanding and potential for theoretical enhancements. Therefore, qualitative methods were chosen for the interpretative nature of the research question and case study. The induction and recursion of empirical instances required an appropriate methodological approach. With a growing interest and discussion on big data and AI within services, a case study and empirical research on customer service advisors and change within their tasks is a coherent and pivotal research question. Ethical approval was established prior to all stages of research.

Equation 2: Customer Retention Model (CR)

$$CR = \theta \cdot (BD_{loyalty\_patterns}) + \kappa \cdot (GA_{engagement\_impact})$$

Where:

- CR = Customer Retention

- $BD_{loyalty\_patterns}$ = Big Data-based loyalty patterns, such as frequency of purchases or historical customer behavior

- $GA_{engagement\_impact}$ = AI-driven engagement, such as loyalty offers or targeted campaigns

- θ, κ = Weights for Big Data loyalty patterns and AI engagement impact

6.4.1. Data Collection and Analysis Techniques

Qualitative Research Methods We conducted twenty in-depth, semi-structured interviews within our participating organizations. A large food retailer and a public sector organization contributed ten interviewees in total from a range of departments. Their roles are outlined in a table. All interview participants had existing interaction with, or knowledge of, customer communications. The ability of the interviews to gather nuanced and detailed insights became clear during data analysis and is reflected in the results in a section. Our sample for the public sector organization also included three focus groups looking at a range of service functions within the same organization. There were five participants in each of these focus groups. In addition to this, a small-scale survey was also completed within our available resources.

6.4.2. Case Study Design

Several reasons justify the choice of these real-life examples. GA applications are numerous nowadays, and the main idea is to present and discuss these cases without pretending to have a complete understanding or in-depth analyses of them. The two different cases satisfy the cases of SAP and Frey and Osborne, but also Boys, Barley, Wilson, Syed, and Solyomi, which consider the consequences on jobs. To collect all the necessary data, the main sources are interviews with company managers and document reviews. The use of a combination of documental analysis and interviews is designed to support triangulation. The cross-examination of different types of sources supports the aim of enriching minds regarding the differences between what managers say and the corporation's goals considering the analysis of the structure. These research methods also permit the collection of longitudinal data to measure trends and change the customer experience. Because the companies are not fully representative and, most of all, not generalizable, the cases cannot discredit extant theories but can support the building of new ones.

6.5. Case Studies

In 2014, Vodafone Group realized how big data can be used to create richer, more immersive personalized marketing experiences using emotional triggers. The group conducted a multi-center neuroscientific investigation of the impact of engaging with cinema. This project was the world's largest comparative study of brain responses to the second-by-second characteristics of films and brand content within those films, which gave a truly global perspective. The research concluded that emotional stimulation was a critical differentiator, with the results being applied across Vodafone markets in Europe, Africa, and India. In the two-week period following the London premiere, Vodafone experienced a 4 percent increase in ad recall and a 2 percent increase in brand perception with a corresponding 25 percent uplift in the quality of interactions. The findings overcome the limitations of traditional types of measurement such as focus groups or self-report surveys. They provide concrete evidence of how branding within the film can evoke strong emotions and cement memories of our products and services, leading to a significant commercial prize.

6.5.1. Successful Implementations of Big Data and Generative AI

Several leaders across industries were interviewed to outline where their firms have successfully implemented big data along with generative AI. These case studies illustrate how a firm approached the strategies and the methods of broader customer experience strategy. Some firms were already publishing numbers through metrics around the customer experience. However, this was always a co-innovation and thus, their competitive advantage. When American businesses are customer experience thought leaders developing the CX measurement methodology and capturing the voice of the customer, results fascinate. The strategy and customer-centric culture show the innovation in the marketplace. A best practice for staying ahead of the customer service curve as the marketplace evolves is to anticipate their needs, rather than react to them. To win in the next horizon in talent, firms will need to start tapping into generative AI to create truly remarkable customer service experiences. The key factor to identify in these case studies is the relationship between these technologies and the brand and customer experience at those brands. To be successful, the use of generative AI must live in partnership with branding.

6.6. Challenges and Future Directions

Though highly promising and expected to develop further, this approach is fraught with many challenges. Compliance with data protection and privacy regulatory frameworks is a primary constraint. Data regulations strictly prohibit undertaking activities such as data harvesting without user consent. Consequently, companies can only collect a limited amount of data regarding their customers, hence still dealing with small data—the same challenge is relevant to generative AI. While we are yet to experience challenges that might emerge in using generative AI in the enhancement of user experience, one of these issues is the potential for illegal or unethical uses. Some ethical, social, or safety challenges might emerge in the future, especially regarding discrimination.

Overall, the study shows that big data—analytics platform integration will enhance the customer experience. We believe this successfully demonstrated how current research and practices can provide useful and in-depth knowledge to practitioners on the potential encountered and unanticipated results of using big data analytics for enhancing customer experience. Additionally, researchers can use these findings to direct future research efforts. Finally, the study's significance, limitations, and potential future research directions are discussed. As previously mentioned, AI is only starting to become formally used for consumer cognition and decision-making technologies; the same applies to AI strategies. This offers promising opportunities for future collaborative activities. Businesses should also adjust their policies and strategies to rely on these new technologies with regard to rapid technology developments.

Equation 3: Customer Experience ROI (CE-ROI)

$$CE - ROI - \frac{Benefit_{CX}}{Cost_{BD} + Cost_{GA}}$$

Where:

- $CE - ROI$ = Customer Experience Return on Investment

- $Benefit_{CX}$ = The benefits accrued from improved customer experience (e.g., increased sales, loyalty, customer satisfaction)

- $Cost_{BD}$ = Costs associated with Big Data (e.g., data storage, analytics tools)

- $Cost_{GA}$ = Costs related to implementing Generative AI (e.g., development of models, infrastructure)

6.6.1. Ethical Considerations

Concern has been raised about the power asymmetries that result from data collection practices. From a corporate perspective, transparency and trust in a company's usage of data are key to customers' willingness to share information. Transparency can create customer convenience if companies highlight upfront which data they collect, for what purposes, and with whom they might share it. Large-scale processing could produce skewed results due to issues of bias or processes that would more frequently resemble the collective and thus the dominant cultural norms. Technically, it seems impossible to anticipate all types of content in advance and provide clear evidence that there is no harmful content among them. These unintended and potential consequences might have far-reaching implications for customer trust.

6.6.2. Potential Innovations and Developments

Innovations can create new data and the necessary input for further service or allocation adaptations. Service coproduction was approached in a predictive manner along with the monitored creation of data to justify short-, medium---, or long-term strategy delivery innovative solutions. The user is the first responsible for the next stage of change and, thus, companies cannot easily predict future customer needs and transformations. With proactive attention to predictive and changing new user needs, in complex processes, alloyed big data and generative AI can ultimately help in a more flexible and sustainable service/product distribution. Digital information leads to global trends and contextual changes that we need to constantly monitor and valorize/share within an extended collaboration that is permanently driven by creativity and proactive responsibility. A variety of innovative programs in big data and generative AI are and will be emerging based on specific applications. The production of empiric data on service design aspects reveals a certain adherence to these emerging trends as the study progressed over time indicating that organizations are actually increasingly concerned about the technological performance of the used tools and their consistency with future service-based innovation directions. The devotion to predictive analysis and proactive-based neurological, emotional, and motivational operations is found through the involvement of future users from the early ideation stages. At the same time, the clear massive responsibilities that the user and organization share need to be deeply changed and reflected further. As such, we will further develop this basic framework of dedicated collaborations in order to develop an augmented model that will illustrate how overall technology itself should only be focused on customers and the wonderfully enlarged network/meaning that it creates.

6.7. Conclusion

This research essay investigates the game-changing potential of Big Data and Generative AI to enhance customer experiences. Data is already reshaping how businesses know and engage with their customers. Interpreting data insights and acting quickly is becoming important to stay relevant. Businesses have already adopted data strategies at some level. For example, tune business operating models, especially retail chains, that rely on analyzing data to decide on shelf layout and product promotions. Big Data means that businesses can execute more extensive strategies for engagements and servicing. However, leaders continue to grapple with transforming big data insights into valuable company assets, primarily extracting customer insights.

Overall, the transition to using AI and Big Data insights for marketing does not come without its caveats, with the main one being the change to organizational functions and training. The field of marketing will see more students and practitioners embark on this journey in the future. Future research directions should evaluate how businesses are using AI and Big Data insights for customer engagement, considering demographics. Future studies may also consider international compliance with data privacy and the specifics of how marketing professionals can keep AI marketing strategies transparent and compliant to avoid fraud and the misuse of client data.

6.7.1. Future Trends

Notes for managerial implications: Big Data and Generative AI will have an influence on business-customer interactions in the upcoming years. Businesses will greatly benefit from understanding these trends and starting to adapt their data-gathering techniques and AI tools to build a competitive advantage. They will need to follow the trends to remain successful in the space of customer journeys and experiences. They will also need to take any ethical concerns raised by privacy-seeking individuals into account in accordance with privacy acts. The same is true for concerns about the societal implications, which can be amplified by the discussed advancements. The Future. We expect even more potential advancements. The themes addressed expect data to be more "interconnected" than it currently is.

References

[1]Ransbotham, S., Kiron, D., & Prentice, P. (2018). Artificial intelligence in business: The state of AI adoption and its future potential. MIT Sloan Management Review.

[2]Shapiro, J. H., & Dudley, B. (2022). Business growth through AI-powered innovation. Journal of Innovation Management, 13(2), 256-267.

[3]Sharma, A., & Gupta, V. (2019). Strategic impact of AI on organizational success: A systematic literature review. Journal of Organizational Change Management, 32(3), 299-320. https://doi.org/10.1108/JOCM-12-2018-0340

[4]Srinivasan, R., & Ray, P. (2020). Big data and AI for growth: The new competitive advantage. Business Strategy Review, 21(4), 74-85. https://doi.org/10.1016/j.bushor.2019.05.004

[5]Subramanian, S., & Lingam, S. (2021). Machine learning and AI in business: Unlocking new growth paths. Springer.

7

The Intersection of Big Data and AI in Supply Chain Optimization

7.1. Introduction

Digital supply chain systems integrate and optimize three key aspects, namely, a full view of logistics activities, integration of the value chain, and adaptation of the network to the competitive environment. Traditional supply chains (SC) are oriented around operational simplification in response to well-defined and stable levels of supply and demand, whereas technologies such as big data and machine-learning-based analytics are fundamentally adapting to the development and management of global supply chains. Advanced production planning and detailed scheduling are being significantly altered in the context of big data prompting predictive demand-based replenishment from full information flows. The supply chain orientation for digital ecosystems with deeply integrated innovation processes goes beyond simple channel management. The degree of supply chain digitization and resulting flexibility to change in logistics and network adaptation are correlated with revenue growth, especially within smaller companies.

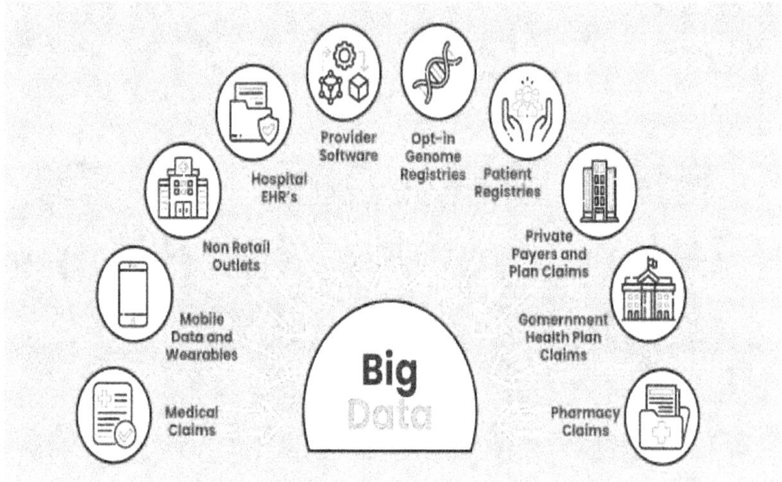

Fig 7.1: Intersection of Big Data and A

7.2. Foundations of Big Data and AI in Supply Chain Management

Big data and analytics are further promising in the management of supply chain operations. Much has been written about using these technologies to make the supply chain more efficient, possibly by resolving inefficiencies or reallocating stock. Freight analytics, utilizing such big data technologies, can track actual ship locations and create the most efficient transshipment routes at each port. However, the supply chain and broader AI can be adjusted to build more responsive demand chains for consumer preferences and seasonal variations based on predictive analytics. Broadly applicable AI technology for supply chain optimization is supported by big data. These effective supply chain management techniques require a large, complex machine learning algorithm and therefore are not practical before the development of cloud computing. Rather than focusing on this loss of potential, which looks difficult at a problem, managers should turn their attention to quantifiable insights. In a similar vein, digital twins are essentially a hyper-accurate format for predictive analytics that utilizes real-time big data feeds. Thus, in the integration of real-time data from big data systems and AI logistics infrastructure, digital twin models can help managers predict future states.

Equation 1: Demand Forecasting using AI (Machine Learning Model)

$$\hat{y}_t = \alpha + \beta_1 x_{1,t-1} + \beta_2 x_{2,t-1} + \cdots + \beta_n x_{n,t-1} + \epsilon_t$$

Where:

- $\hat{y}_t$ = predicted demand at time t

- α = intercept

- $\beta_1, \beta_2, \ldots, \beta_n$ = coefficients for independent variables

- $x_{i,t-1}$ = values of variables (e.g., past sales, economic indicators) at time $t - 1$

- ϵ_t = error term

7.2.1. Big Data in Supply Chain Management

Big data and its analysis help drive business operations, including supply chain management. Supply chains typically generate large amounts of data covering routine operational transactions such as payments, orders, and transportation. Connectivity between the supply chain, ecosystem, and customers generates vast data like that in social media. The surge of IoT devices lends one more level of connectivity to supply chain data. Big data analytics is useful for better prediction and risk control, and the shared insights will lead to better decision-making. Technologies and tools are used in managing big data. Real-time supply chain analytics can facilitate quicker responses to changes and risks, strengthening supply chain agility or the capability to adapt to such changes. Forecasting capability is improved when decision-makers understand the variables internal and external to their operations. Organizations that understand consumer sentiments, trends, and market conditions, and adjust product promotions, supplies, and deliveries have found better and more agile supply chains. Analytics are used on multiple data sets that are proliferating as organizations aim to extract more value. While the cost-effectiveness of big data analytics is continuously improving, the major issue that arises is the overload of data. Up-to-date toolsets and qualified employees are other issues to be addressed. There are instances of hyper-competitive global markets. A company states that its data resources encompass a significant amount of information that flows through its metroplexes daily. The company captures a large amount of real-time data from its scanned barcodes that help respond to alterations in the goods it is moving. Another company is using big data to comprehend areas such as road conditions and vehicle information among other data benefits. In business-to-consumer supply chains, data availability greatly multiplied as companies captured and distributed data to suppliers and partners in the past decades. The quantity of data available for analysis was growing exponentially. Big data is poised to dominate supply chain management now and in the near future and serve as the foundation for adding artificial intelligence to supply chain applications.

7.2.2. AI Techniques in Supply Chain Optimization

Big Data and AI in Supply Chain Management 2.2. AI Techniques in Supply Chain Optimization There is a range of AI techniques, such as machine learning, natural language processing, and computer vision, which have emerged in recent decades and gained significant traction due to their potential for developing various applications relevant to AI techniques. Among all the AI techniques, machine learning is one of the prominent methods as it can automatically identify the underlying patterns in a dataset. Unlike traditional statistical concepts, wherein the relationship among the different variables is defined a priori, a machine learning model is capable of learning this relationship during the model optimization process. Hence, machine learning is particularly useful for making predictions. With the help of machine learning algorithms, it learns from historical data and makes predictions about the future. Moreover, in cases where you cannot explicitly program a solution, machine learning is used—for example, in cases where a large number of decision variables are connected, using extensive data to describe the relationships among the variables.

7.3. Applications of Big Data and AI in Supply Chain Optimization

Delving into the ways big data intersects with AI to enable swift, data-driven decisions in the supply chain, let's explore a few examples in more depth: Demand Forecasting: Big data analytics employs historical data, real-time feeds, social listening, and geo-data, along with external data feeds to evaluate patterns in demand. This method provides a more credible alternative to traditional forecasting models, as it uses additional data to predict customer buying patterns based on accurate indicators. Inventory Management: Inventory management software can forecast customer needs and automate orders that update in real time. This means that, when integrated with suppliers' own systems, businesses can make real-time adjustments based on seconds-long updates on customer inventory. This not only reduces the costs associated with maintaining inventory but also increases customer satisfaction by minimizing stockouts on essential and in-demand items. Transportation Optimization: Using big data, algorithms can calculate the best routes for all deliveries across third-party logistics, carriers, and pre-built platforms to determine the best vehicle and event staging for delivery and collection. This process optimizes and decreases costs associated with the logistics of the supply chain, from road and ocean freight to last-mile delivery trucks. The bottom line won't shock you: the melding of big data and AI has the ability to provide companies with a competitive advantage in the supply chain. Having systems in place to predict and act on customer needs somewhere between 70% to 80% more accurately than a company that doesn't have big data in its toolkit is a major market differentiator. Consequently, firms have the potential to leverage big data analytics to conduct business at a much finer level of economic efficiency than would otherwise be possible.

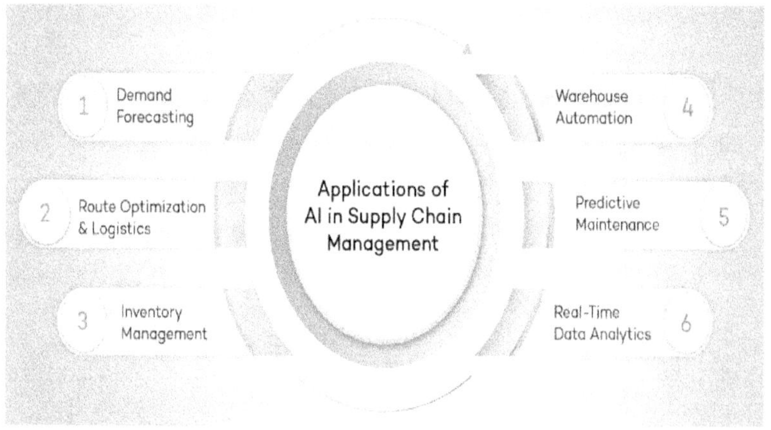

Fig 7.2: Applications of AI in Supply Chain Management

7.3.1. Demand Forecasting

Despite more powerful hardware systems and software applications to process vast amounts of data, traditional human prediction is limited because the data size still exceeds human capability. With the size of data able to be handled by modern computer systems, demand forecasts have a high propensity to be more accurate. Logistically, companies benefit from forecast accuracy regarding lowering costs, maintaining order cycle times, enhancing performance, and aspiring for effect as well as reducing the amount of inventory on hand to improve inventory turnovers. When a forecast is inaccurate, there are several ways companies can safeguard against the implications. One is by adjusting the forecast as frequently as possible to promote more accurate forecasts. Another way is through implementing more advanced analytics to determine the appropriate best-value sources. Equally, supply chain firms need to invest more time and resources into becoming more collaborative to promote more accurate forecasts.

7.3.2. Inventory Management

Inventory management plays a critical role in any supply chain; any poor decisions within this function can result in either high inventory or low inventory. Overstocking increases costs in terms of money locked in inventory and maintenance costs, and stock outs also cost in terms of sales opportunities lost. Big data can help organizations achieve accuracy in data and make data-driven decisions in real-time or near real-time to avoid unnecessary costs. With big data, the organization can analyze sales patterns to determine appropriate inventory levels, while the inventory level is affected by the performance of suppliers. Real-time big data analytics can provide insights into inventory holding, thereby reducing inventory costs. AI can provide great insights into this type of problem.

There are different AI technologies, such as machine learning tools and demand planning software, which take big data and help spot sales trends. Also, AI-enhanced selection requirement tools, such as intelligent robotic process automation systems, and AI applications provide predictive insights that inform the decisions of when to reorder lead time. AI uses sales and procurement data to optimize the inventory turnover rate. When using big data to optimize inventory management processes, AI-equipped predictive analytics support lead demand to identify when inventory needs to be replenished, offering a production forecast or predicting seasonal behavior and external factors. Then the plan predicts when demand for the product will be high or low most of the time and estimates how many of the product will be sold in each future period. AI can provide information about the relevant inventory levels to meet customer demand.

7.3.3. Transportation Optimization

Big data analytics is an approach that deals with employing a plethora of massively parallel, distributed architectures to handle an unprecedented load of data. In the case of transportation, these architectures allow for the analysis of models and comparison of their predictions in a reasonable time. Big data analytics can be used in transportation optimization to use historical traffic data to analyze traffic patterns in different locations, identify optimal driving routes, optimize delivery timelines, optimize traffic signal patterns, and curb traffic congestion. AI consists of computer software that adapts its operations to the pure number-crunching input flowing through it. AI can enhance the big data analytics-driven insight to provide a more in-depth impact analysis. Optimization algorithms used in AI can both decrease vehicle congestion and improve traffic flow. These can also assist with fleet management and calculated routing by providing better support for planning optimization and forecast modeling. In transportation optimization, vehicles are another model element. While individual vehicles cannot be modeled, small artificial intelligence within the optimization algorithm can adjust vehicle routing to these conditions up to five changes in the numerical values for each vehicle batch, nationwide, for a week in a matter of minutes. Each optimization algorithm also provides a comparison of how some of the inputs are managed in real time, such as fleet management, dynamic routing, fuel consumption, and delivery times.

7.4. Challenges and Future Directions

While the future holds great potential for the intersection of big data and AI in supply chain optimization, there are also several barriers that need to be addressed. By its nature, big data holds the potential to expose sensitive information that needs to be kept private and secure; this tension is particularly acute in supply chain organizations that have developed highly confidential supply bases. Data governance and other compliance issues also raise concerns over who is able to access, manage, and utilize data at different milestones along the supply chain. Another complex issue surrounds the integration of technical systems and expertise, such as planning systems utilized by strategists and other AI tools used by operators on the ground. To enhance supply chain systems, supply organizations will also have to increase their capacity to integrate these two types of IT infrastructure.

Equation 2: Inventory Optimization (Economic Order Quantity - EOQ)

$$EOQ - \sqrt{\frac{2DS}{H}}$$

Where:

- D = demand rate (units per period)

- S = ordering cost per order

- H = holding cost per unit per period

7.4.1. Data Privacy and Security Concerns

Supply chains generate and process large amounts of sensitive data, including customer information, financial and transaction details, employee and workforce information, supplier details, operational information, demand information, and production and delivery schedules. Data obtained from social networks and the internet identifies behavioral patterns that could belong to individuals. Data breaches or unauthorized access can lead to misuse of such data, and companies are accountable to their stakeholders for such risks and for failing to prevent and protect such data. Furthermore, it is observed that reasons for data breaches can be internal: malicious or unauthorized data access, theft by employees, or human errors. Therefore, a culture of vigilance and protection mechanisms needs to be developed to prevent data leakages. The protection and security of supply chain data affect the other two critical areas of supply chain operations, namely AI and blockchain. The fraud detection behavioral models also require the sharing of data over a secured network for training AI or deep learning models that could suppress fraud.

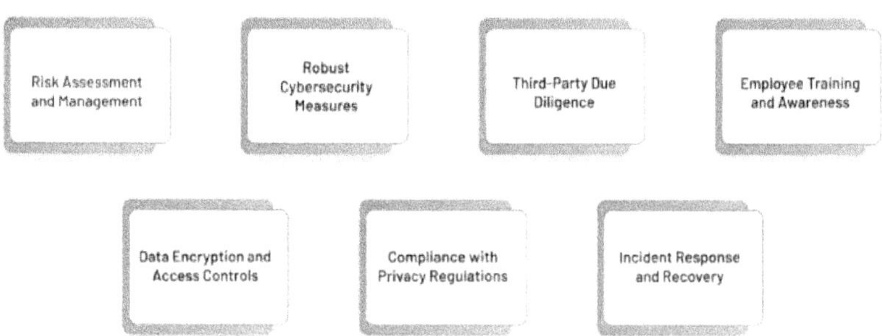

Fig 7.3: Data Security and Privacy

7.4.2. Integration of Big Data and AI Technologies

This implies that many legacy systems are still used for planning and operational aspects. In particular, these systems concentrate on designing methods and physical network distribution mechanisms, optimization techniques, pricing, and reliability methods; limited or no use of AI, deep learning, natural language processing, robotics, and IoT is considered. Manufacturing and logistics firms that cannot afford to migrate to the cloud for intelligent manufacturing strategies must close the IT operation and supply chain disconnect. Thus, for instance, building a new, scalable IT infrastructure, applications, and surveillance systems must be prioritized. Moreover, it is essential to adopt open technology standards and collaborate with IT groups within the organization, as well as the chief digitization, transformation, operations, and supply chain executives, to develop a coherent changeover years before it becomes critical. Management teams should transfer competencies toward a hybrid-cloud strategy and develop capacities that can drive this organizational shift. Taking advantage of the advances in IoT sensors, big data platforms, and machine learning/artificial intelligence technological and functional capabilities, may require the use of a converged infrastructure that consists of IT, manufacturing, and operational management.

7.4.3. Ethical Implications

As with any new technology, the implementation of big data and AI applications raises several ethical implications. Taken broadly, these implications relate primarily to transparency and accountability in automated decision-making processes. There is a need to address the discrimination in outcomes that inevitably occurs when decisions are based on historical data. In addition to lacking transparency, AI and ML models can be influenced by data drift, whereby the data used in building the learning model becomes misaligned with current observational trends. The issue of algorithmic bias is well documented. Widespread discussion has centered around translating established ethical principles into guidelines in order to address these challenges. Ethical guidelines developed by professional bodies take a coercive stance, in that developers should follow professional obligations. Others opt for a permissive approach, which equips developers and organizations to proactively address damage before it occurs. Approximately half of the emerging literature calls for externally developed regulations and guidelines.

This section aims to raise awareness about the ethical challenges associated with the deployment of big data and AI in supply chain management. By demonstrating these ethical implications in detail, the section aims to stimulate discussion about how organizations should proceed in their quest for an optimized supply chain.

Equation 3: Supply Chain Network Optimization (Transportation Problem)

$$\text{Minimize} \quad Z - \sum_{i=1}^{m} \sum_{j=1}^{n} c_{ij} x_{ij}$$

Where:

- c_{ij} = cost of transporting one unit from supplier i to customer j

- x_{ij} = number of units to be transported from supplier i to customer j

- m = number of suppliers

- n = number of customers

7.5. Conclusion

In this paper, we have reviewed the modern trends in Big Data and AI technologies. We focused on the intersection of Big Data and AI in supply chain optimization, which we could deduce that the amounts of studies dealing with this area are increasing year by year. By the analysis, we can conclude that the Big Data and AI technologies transformations are too significant in human decisions and involved directly in the efficiency of organizations. In our case, the impact of AI and Big Data technologies on supply chain optimization could also be concluded as important as another area. However, it can also be interpreted as speculative. It is necessary to pay attention to the questions we don't know about what we don't know. Towards the future and the future of data-driven competitive advantage, we believe it is also very important to follow AI trends and technologies in planning activities. As seen in the results, the concepts of Big Data and AI with supply chain and optimization areas have been evaluated by qualitative and quantitative studies. The publication of studies has increased relatively in recent years, especially in 2017, 2019, and 2020. However, keeping up with changing technologies and moving from existing opportunities to developing trends is a problem if organizations do not act quickly. Although the use of these technologies has not yet become widespread, it is necessary to constantly improve and expand these technologies, so that every organization can assess its existing situation and possible investments in this regard, to create an economic rationale for the optimal cost involved. It is not necessary for organizations to make investments because they do not yet have the necessary knowledge and experience, but it is enough to act quickly and to enable organizations and decision-makers to act when it is necessary to invest in these technologies.

7.5.1. Future Trends

In the future, several technological advances are expected to shape supply chain optimization further: the emergence of autonomous systems for solving supply chain managerial problems is expected to revolutionize typical replenishment logistics operations. These emerging optimal autonomous logistic applications understandably increase reliance on accurate data, hence the increased demand for solutions that can handle large data generated in enterprise resource planning or advanced planning systems. Other trends, such as real-time supply chains and the need for real-time decision-making systems, are important as modern supply chains try to become more agile. This implies predictive capabilities of big data analytics to provide early warning signs of production failures or sudden distribution channel shifts that may require rapid alterations in operational and logistics flows. A third trend— blockchain-based information sharing—pertains to data and supply chain traceability and transparency and may help mitigate supply chain risk by fostering proactive risk management. The development and advances in both government regulation and industrial practice are promoting multiple applications of AI technologies to be introduced into many different areas, for example, fintech, industrial big data, and autonomous driving. Recently, many countries around the world also started to enforce regulatory compliance of AI by developing new regulations in the areas of AI ethics, explaining AI decisions, and further technical guidance in part of models and risk management systems for new sectors as and when they emerge.

References

[1] Tene, O., & Polonetsky, J. (2020). Big data for business leaders. Springer.

[2]Uren, B., & Smith, S. (2019). Generative AI applications in business strategy. Journal of Business Strategy, 41(5), 62-71. https://doi.org/10.1108/JBS-04-2019-0101

[3]Verma, P., & Agarwal, A. (2022). Harnessing the power of big data for organizational growth. Technology Innovation Management Review, 12(6), 34-45.

[4]Ward, M., & McDonald, M. (2021). The future of business success through big data. Business Intelligence Journal, 26(3), 159-174.

[5]Westerman, G., & Calméjane, C. (2018). Digital transformation: A roadmap for billion-dollar organizations. MIT Press.

8

Ethical and Legal Considerations in Big Data and Generative AI Utilization

8.1. Introduction

In a world of budding scientific and technical feats, the questions of "should we" and "what are the wider implications" of the innovation should be as consequential as the ubiquitous "can we." This statement for the record aims to explore the importance of this subject regarding big data and generative AI so society may prudently consider issues related to running hand-in-hand with these paramount questions. In fact, the ethical implications of developing these technologies seem to be boundless; from preventing malignant brain disorders to leaping over the abyss of razor-thin margin winning in the derivatives market. Cognitive computing systems utilizing big data could conceivably emulate a person; imagine the transformative potential in healthcare—therapeutics, analyses, epidemiological advancements, and development aid. In criminal justice and policy making, AI might deliver insights into risk and intervention for recidivists. Like humans, generative AI performs new thought by analyzing novel data from the combination of two datasets. Ethically, there are equal benefits and challenges, opportunities presenting new legal developments to actualize an old rule of wise limitation into everyday society. Ethical or not, nations across our planet are

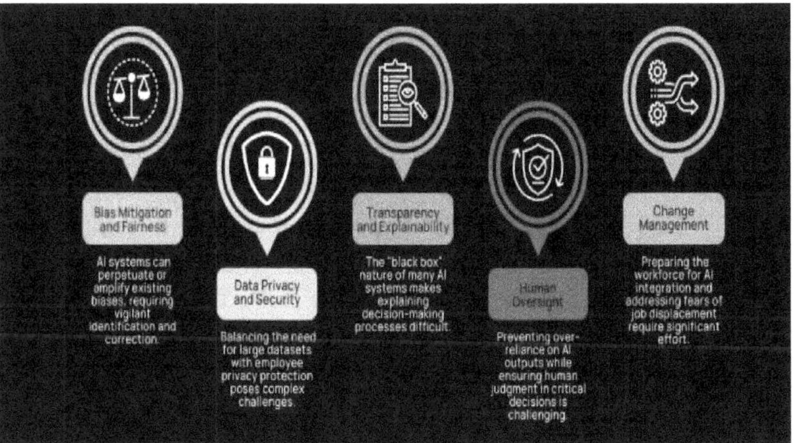

embracing the twin cognitions in terrific fervor—to the tune of billion-dollar investments transnationally.

Fig 8.1: Ethical Considerations of Generative AI

8.1.1. Background and Significance

In recent years, significant technological advancements have led to the evolution of large-scale big data and data-driven decision-making processes in various industrial, commercial, social, and other disciplines. Practically, large-scale data and big data innovations empower vital applications like predictive analysis in healthcare, finance, agriculture, business intelligence, machine learning, profit and non-profit organizations, etc. Advanced analytics and machine learning depend on the available data to test correlations among parameters and utilize these correlations to predict or optimize future outcomes. In addition, techniques such as generative and adaptive network-based models are capable of learning from data and mimicking existing patterns, behaviors, and features of the underlying system, a technology known by multiple names. As a result, as data-driven operations and decision-making processes consider routine operations and enterprises, it is time to rethink the possible misuse of such technologies and develop mechanisms to safeguard against these potentialities.

8.1.2. Purpose of the Study

At this stage, our current findings can help to raise awareness and place some normative limits, particularly on generative AI, but also on AI that can benefit from the use of big data. Nonetheless, our proposals will need to be gradually adjusted as new technological and societal phenomena either unfold or mature. We emphasize that our main scope in this study is not on establishing whether current legislation is capable of restraining the negative impacts of AI based on particularly big data, but primarily on the analysis of the reasons preventing or limiting their compliance. The main objective is to address this issue as an early indication of the big data and generative AI ethical considerations, rather than to systematically arrive at the conclusions that should mark a compliance audit. We focus here on the obvious and largely underestimated initial assumption of the difficulty of fitting these two emerging, rather odd, technologies—big data and generative AI—within the established framework of legislation, starting with data protection law, competition law, and contracting practices. The section then takes a broader look at these technological innovations and suggests that a broad ethical basis analysis can be helpful pending an ethical and legislative convergence approach. In our study, we discuss big data without turning our attention to profiling and behavioral targeting, as these topics have been particularly addressed.

8.2. Big Data and Generative AI Overview

Most narrow and artificial AI machines are programmed to do a defined task without explicitly being programmed step by step. They are also not only able to perform a single task, which can lack adaptability, giving them 'limited intelligence' as they are specialized in only one field. Big data serves as input to train AI and machine learning algorithms to learn from the massive amount of data to improve decision-making, reducing false positives in detection and regulatory compliance and responsibility for more of society's decisions. High-powered AI and data-analytic software can analyze more and more data with growing velocity, uncovering more patterns and masses of information. As such, these technologies have significant transformative potential within finance, retail, marketing, healthcare, criminal justice, education, and employment among others.

Generative AI is the subset of machine learning algorithms designed to imitate human artistic output containing characteristics like creativity, surprise, and emotional reaction. The results output from generative AI techniques include easy-to-process elements and materials such as images or music, along with the complexity of public opinion and copyright. A definition could include computers generating content that is generally considered the result of human creative processes. Artificial creativity has been recognized as a distinct field of AI since the 1990s, and general techniques for generative models have existed since the early 1970s.

Equation 1: Privacy Risk Equation

$$R_{privacy} = f(D_{sensitive}, P_{protection}, C_{context})$$

Where:

- $R_{privacy}$ = Privacy risk (higher value means higher risk)

- $D_{sensitive}$ = Amount of sensitive or personal data involved

- $P_{protection}$ = Level of data protection (e.g., encryption, anonymization)

- $C_{context}$ = Context in which data is used (e.g., business use, public sharing)

8.2.1. Definition and Conceptual Frameworks

The common standard and definition of ethical implications in the big data management toolkit adopts two definitions: a definition of big data and a definition of generative AI. Big data refers to data exploring a wide range of organizational and unstructured types from internal and external sources and is usually intertemporal. There are some key dimensions and characteristics differentiating between ordinary data and big data utilized for further analysis, including velocity, variety, and volume. Traditionally, private sectors, knowledge-based entities, and state institutions focused on significant varieties of quantifiable information, manifested through binary or multi-polynomial numerical occurrences that are easy and accurate to manage and analyze. Nonetheless, collecting and analyzing this data is complex and costly, particularly with large volumes. This is one of the key reasons why a new branch of science called data examination, or big data analysis, has emerged to change and improve analysis within this field.

Two main dimensions need to be noted: first, the volume and variety context specifies that there is little or no control over collecting and producing big data due to its diverse sources and volume due to the pretext of operating in a retirement economy. This means that standard storage and analysis solutions do not apply in this context or must be rigorously adjusted. Data is mostly connected to current and prospective interactions between millions of people and a number of programming systems underpinning the operations of retirement exchange organizations. The importance of this characteristic highlights the risks associated with the conduct and behaviors related to the right to privacy and data protection, as well as risks associated with the theory of large numbers, albeit in small cases. Owing to the size of this data, the international society seems to be reanalyzing its uses and risks. Second, when big data operates through generative AI systems emerging from the field of generative modeling in deep learning, it is released from the previous analytical ends of big data. This creates a novel functionality that generates new data files and releases deep data applications and path-breaking techniques by widening the universe of big data analysis. These points stress that the framework underpinning the standard seems to be theoretically sound, despite real disagreements that continue to spark heated debate both legally and ethically. Understanding this is crucial to understanding the discussions held later.

8.2.2. Applications and Use Cases

Big data and generative AI have vast and diverse applications and use cases in the industry. One of the most popular use cases of big data relates to analytics: big data can be used to provide advanced and predictive analytics as companies gather data from predictive models and other data sources to identify trends. Data-driven marketing is a major use case of this phenomenon. A second use case is the development of personalized medicine that fits drug types based on a patient's genetics; genomics offers a window into personalized medicine that big data can utilize. It can also identify patterns in health and disease by using data to provide predictive analytics. Big data analysis is widespread in the finance sector as well; it is used to flag fraudulent activities and streamline stock trading. Generative AI can automate content generation and can also be used to replicate the human hand in creating images.

By placing the power to generate original content in the hands of users, companies facilitate customer involvement, user-generated content, and creativity. Big companies have used this technology to create content on a massive scale. Similarly, predictive analytics using big data from hotels is known to predict the number of customers and preferences of visitors. Big data is the cream of the crop with respect to competitive intelligence and can be used for 360-degree profiling of any entity. These technological advancements have the ability to drastically improve existing products, services, and business models. Providing an immersive experience to customers with the help of detailed knowledge management processes of generative AI game environments can help educate or showcase a product in a controlled environment. All of this should be seen in light of two things: the consumer experience and operational efficiencies. While the benefits of leveraging generative AI are undeniable, ethical questions embedded in these reasonable endeavors are equally significant to consider.

8.3. Ethical Considerations in Big Data and Generative AI

Ethical considerations have arisen from the collection and processing of big data in developed societies. Data availability raises a fundamental privacy question: what information should remain private and unrecorded? In response to this new data availability, international regulations that aim to protect individual privacy against excessive data collection and processing have gained prominence. While data protection reflects the legal implications of data collection, use, and storage, an ethical issue concerning the collection and selling of private data remains. The commodification of personal data and the use of data for profit-making give rise to continuing ethical debates. The main ethical questions of collecting and processing large amounts of data entail: 1) ethical issues concerning advertising, marketing, loyalty, and market segmentation; and 2) operational ethical issues for managers regarding effectively protecting customer information and privacy.

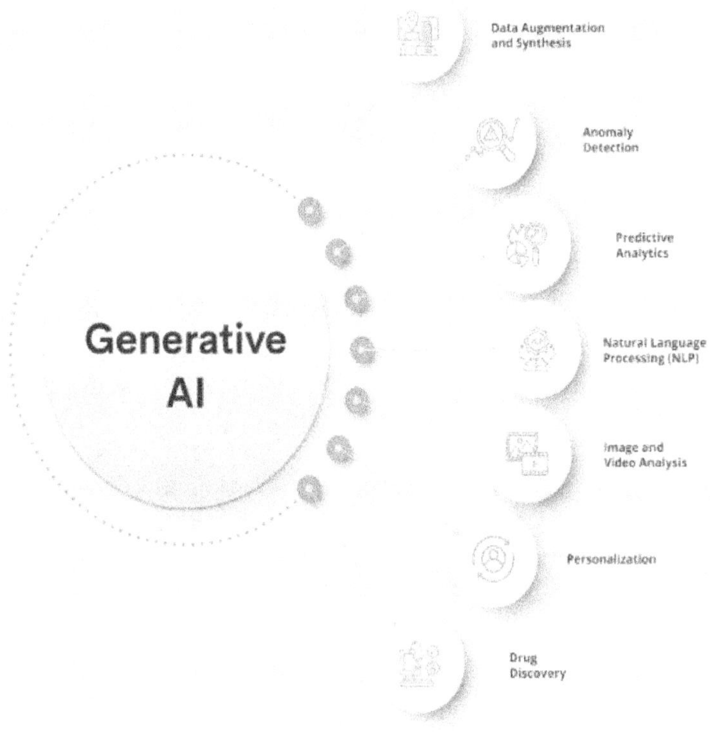

Fig 8.2: Generative AI Data Analysis

8.3.1. Privacy and Data Protection

Data protection and privacy are integral to the operation of both big data and generative AI systems. Politics, trade secrets, financial reports, private health information, and law enforcement data are extremely sensitive and should be kept confidential from unauthorized access. Failing to maintain privacy may result in reputational damage, financial loss, betrayal of trust, or other harm. Additionally, unauthorized use or spread of generated data may cause significant harm. Moreover, individuals do not want their data to be used in modeling or generating information without their knowledge.

Unsavory activities, disdain from related groups, and harm to personal and professional reputations can easily arise from the generation of art that is contrary to an individual's aesthetic. When generating instances in specialized and unanticipated contexts, small, dissimilar, and de-identified datasets that pose lower risk are not as easy to obtain and incorporate other personal information.

8.3.2. Bias and Fairness

Data used to train AI systems may contain bias. This is particularly problematic when using AI systems that are then left to produce content that is automatically shared with the public. Bias is undesirable because it may reflect historic or systemic discrimination present in the training data. If a recommender system based on generative AI parameters is biased in favor of a particular demographic, it may hurt the feelings of other members of society and risk being seen as unethical. The discussion about AI bias has mainly centered on image recognition algorithms. Some of these can be less accurate when recognizing members of groups that were underrepresented during their initial training than for people of other demographic groups. In the digital full-body scan example, the racist elements in the mirror example reinforce biases present in society at large and are therefore considered unethical by default.

8.3.3. Transparency and Accountability

Transparency and accountability are themes that are increasingly being addressed, particularly with respect to the relevance of big data in law enforcement and customs applications, as well as the effects of data and generative AI on individuals' right to privacy, especially when deployed to enhance surveillance, recognize identities, or create deep fakes. There is an increasing demand, particularly from data subjects, for AI decisions to be explainable. Explainable AI (XAI), especially explanations based on the interaction behavior of the system with the user, are being proposed as methods of showing individuals what information an AI system requires in order to carry out a task. This could allow for the explanation of why a particular individual was selected for inspection.

A case study of the introduction of body scanners at an airport shows how this need for traceability is predicated on expert knowledge being the basis on which policies can be understood and welfare maximized. Data protection authorities also stress the role of transparency in fostering trust. A poll found that the factor most important to an individual in determining whether they can trust an organization was that the organization is serious about protecting personal data.

8.4. Legal Frameworks and Regulations

SECTION 4: Legal Frameworks and Regulations In the past decade, using big data and increasingly generative AI technologies has become prominent in many parts of the global economy. The confluence of legal norms, ethics, and societal norms is crucial given evolving technologies and normative shifts. Traders and stores can leverage vast data banks to predict consumer choices. In public health, the use of algorithms can predict disease outbreaks as well as individual pregnancies with a high degree of accuracy.

Consequently, privacy law is becoming a more hotly discussed topic, and previously rare references to it in trade agreements are becoming increasingly common. However current legal norms are not comprehensive. Ethical guidelines and regulations are a point of reference today in a rapidly evolving field, meant to help organizations and their constituencies chart their compliance strategies and corporate governance outlines. The General Data Protection Regulation has strict regulations giving data subjects a vast array of rights pertaining to data about them and including provisions on the use of AI and potentially automated decision-making. Ethical AI guidelines, several sets of which have been adopted by countries and individual states, tend to embrace AI with an emphasis on public safety and human dignity. Few, if any, existing ethical guidelines appear to impose direct, affirmative obligations on developers or users of AI, and most list recommended practices for how AI should be developed and implemented.

Equation 2: Fairness Equation

$$F_{\text{fairness}} = \frac{\sum |T_{\text{group1}} - T_{\text{group2}}|}{N}$$

Where:

- F_{fairness} = Fairness score (lower is better)

- T_{group1} = Treatment or outcome for group 1 (e.g., racial or gender group)

- T_{group2} = Treatment or outcome for group 2

- N = Total number of groups considered

8.4.1. General Data Protection Regulation (GDPR)

The General Data Protection Regulation (GDPR) represents a regulation by the European Parliament, the Council of the European Union, and the European Commission with the purpose of reinforcing the personal right to data protection and privacy. GDPR was adopted in 2018 and became enforceable in 2019, with the final objective of providing control over one's personal data and simplifying the regulatory environment of international business by unifying the regulation within the European Union. As a result, the GDPR applies as a standard of data processing and management to all organizations that directly process personal data of citizens located within the European Union, and to organizations that transfer personal data outside of the European Union. This makes the GDPR directly applicable and transcends European legislation regarding data protection to regulation of global impact.

8.4.2. Ethical AI Guidelines and Principles

Major International Initiatives The development of AI technologies should always take privacy and data protection rules into account, as well as the principle of equality and the prohibition of discrimination. There are also a number of ethical AI guidelines and principles available, which are generally based on international human rights and aimed at guiding the deployment of principled AI. These ethical AI considerations support a Responsible Research and Innovation perspective. Data protection and privacy regulations also demand an ethics-by-design approach but are, in general, not concerned with very new scenarios such as AI completely automatically creating, owning, managing, and providing access to the generative material it produces, which can be downloaded, reused, modified, and shared by anyone.

8.5. Case Studies and Examples

Various organizations have encountered ethical dilemmas in their use of big data. A promotional mailer was sent to a teenage girl in Minneapolis, advertising baby products and other relevant goods; her father was incensed. The mailer inadvertently revealed to her parents and the data merchant that she was pregnant, even though she had not said anything. This was a secured purchase with a properly used in-house algorithm that could effectively forecast an individual's pregnancy status. Nonetheless, it was an unethical business practice. This case study provides some common pitfalls to avoid with the use of big data - namely, collecting or using data that is intended to be private. It also shows fashion trends beyond bestselling novels and personal search results in big data, portraying how technology businesses should concentrate more on pursuing basic technological principles in ethics and avoid unethical care of data. The case of the teenage girl in Minneapolis highlights a significant ethical dilemma in the use of big data. While the in-house algorithm used by the data merchant was effective in predicting her pregnancy status, the breach of privacy that followed was deeply unethical. This incident underscores the risks of collecting and using data that individuals believe to be private, particularly when it reveals sensitive information without consent. It demonstrates the potential harm that can arise when businesses prioritize data-driven insights over the ethical principles of privacy and transparency. Technology companies must be vigilant in ensuring that their use of big data aligns with fundamental ethical standards, prioritizing the responsible handling of personal data to protect individuals' rights and trust. This case serves as a reminder that businesses should focus not only on technological innovation but also on safeguarding personal information, respecting privacy, and maintaining ethical integrity.

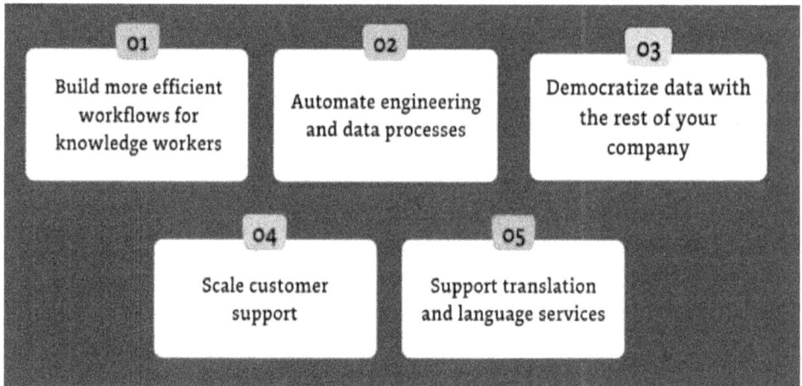

Fig 8.3: Generative AI Use Cases

8.5.1. Ethical Dilemmas in Big Data Utilization

A number of ethical dilemmas arise when organizations begin utilizing big data. For example, an organization wanting to use big data in an effort to identify those most likely to respond to a call for a new life insurance product has reasoned doubts as to whether standardized informed consents were actually valid; a transit corporation with subscription data seeking to utilize that data to begin informing it how to identify those passengers with psychosocial disabilities; a big-box discount retailer wanting to use facial recognition to spot banned shoplifters; a bank wanting to use big data linked to mobile devices to inform it which of two sets of individuals led more stable lives, with the aim of concentrating its own risk on the more plodding ones who are more likely to be able to make repayments.

8.5.2.   Legal   Challenges   in Generative AI

The application of generative AI is accompanied by the emergence of a number of legal challenges. Especially in the context where generative AI is used for content generation or is deployed at the human-AI interface, specific issues relating to liability, copyright, and intellectual property rights arise. One of the core concerns is that legally when generative AI creates outputs, an exigent question is who should bear accountability for those outputs and also who should own the outputs given that generative AI is essentially providing those as a service. Current laws can be read as indicating that the person commissioning the work is the first owner, and there are also initiatives that allow co-ownership between the AI developer and the person commissioning the generative AI as the first owner. In short, the situation is rather complex, and this would need to be addressed by a policy or directive.

Equation 3: Accountability Equation

$$A_{\text{accountability}} = f(T_{\text{transparency}}, A_{\text{auditability}}, R_{\text{responsibility}})$$

Where:

- $A_{\text{accountability}}$ = Accountability score

- $T_{\text{transparency}}$ = Level of transparency (e.g., how much the AI system's decisions can be understood)

- $A_{\text{auditability}}$ = Auditability (e.g., how easy it is to trace and verify decisions made by the AI system)

- $R_{\text{responsibility}}$ = Responsibility (e.g., who is responsible for AI decision outcomes)

8.6. Conclusion

In Chapter 6, we summarized the discussions in Chapters 1 to 5 on how to ethically and legally utilize big data and generative AI and proposed various directions. The purpose of this study is not to make a thorough investigation of the evolving technologies and their implications in society, but rather to start a concerted effort to search for and compare notable ethical codes of big data and AI and report on the results of the private survey. We do not try to present ethical principles or legal rules to which all or most people who work with technologies would agree. Researchers should conduct more investigations with researchers in diverse fields, experimental philosophers, and stakeholders of data and AI themselves in further developing the integrative ethical and legal framework for big data and generative AI utilization. We believe that this is just a starting point and that research should continue to proceed over time. Ethical and legal guidelines will need to continue to be updated as technologies and applications by each new technological platform become lower-cost and ubiquitous for more individuals. If there is too much or too little regulation in the face of the risks above, it can and will be harmful to society. Thus, it is necessary to compare regulations and guidelines multiple times, leveraging the wisdom of policymakers. Hence, researchers must maintain a very objective attitude to continuously update the guidelines in line with the technological levels at the time. In addition, given the expanding usage of big data and generative AI, it should be used for ethical science and open data and collaboration. It is believed that the diversification of input by many stakeholders can facilitate further research. In the future, it would be desirable to consider the inherent positive effects of the use of these technologies.

8.6.1. Future Trends

The technological evolution in the fields of big data and AI is a growing trend and is expected to bring next-generation use cases in numerous economic sectors that could also have beneficial implications for societal values and rights. However, along with those technological advancements come several complex societal challenges, including, but not limited to, ethical and legal challenges, that will have to be discussed and dealt with to ensure advancements in the respective fields occur in a responsible manner. With AI and big data advancing, it also seems likely that future societies may begin to demand new laws and regulations that are capable of keeping up with technological evolution. In this regard, international multi-stakeholder approaches will be essential to reduce ethical and legal uncertainties. A future society may pay attention to whether a business player has the capacity to make AI systems more diverse, privacy-enabling, and fairer by default. In regard to AI technologies, we cannot predict for sure how AI ecosystems will develop in the next 20-30 years, considering their generative capabilities. However, genuinely 'alive' AI, bearing the qualities of the imaginative creation of researchers, could soon be realized in video games, literature, cinema, and various multimedia content productions. Consequently, as of today, there is no imaginable scenario in which legal persons could apply the right to credit AI ecosystems in the near future, as even more advanced AI systems are designed to credit others for their actions and voice and realize themselves. Given the generative potential of AI ecosystems, the new laws relevant to digitality and personhood should also concern the ethical and legal scenarios currently under-focused, as well as the risks of recognizing 'artistic authorship' to AI ecosystems.

References

[1]Wilson, H. J., & Daugherty, P. R. (2018). Collaborative intelligence: Humans and AI are joining forces. Harvard Business Review Press.

[2]Xu, X., & Tan, W. (2021). Big data analytics and AI for transforming organizational capabilities. Journal of Digital Innovation, 8(2), 111-122.

[3]Yates, J., & Martin, M. (2020). The evolving role of AI in driving business scalability. AI and Business Innovation, 7(3), 120-135.

[4]Yu, L., & Xiao, T. (2022). The role of generative AI in enhancing business value. AI Research Journal, 24(4), 222-237. https://doi.org/10.1016/j.aiq.2022.02.004

[5]Zeng, R., & Xie, L. (2021). Unlocking value with big data and AI: Strategic insights and growth opportunities. Journal of Strategic Technology, 9(5), 49-62.

9

Scaling Growth Through Big Data and Generative AI Integration

9.1. Introduction

The age of big data and generative AI has arrived. The companies that will thrive in the digital economy are going to be those who embrace and understand the in-depth principles underpinning big data and generative AI. At a fundamental level, all they have to do is leverage massive amounts of digital capabilities. When done carefully, the nuances invisible to the human eye can be used to buttress everything from the bottom line to managerial effectiveness to operational metrics. Big data has created the capability to turn organizations into data-driven entities, meaning they can understand their functioning, processes, and possibilities of enhancing efficiency via detailed analysis of operational details. Generative AI is revolutionizing the way businesses make decisions, big and small. Due to their increasing importance, the combination of big data and generative AI has been leveraged at the stage of exploratory analytics for several business applications.

Fig 9.1: Scaling Generative AI

9.1.1. Background and Significance

The proliferation of powerful big data technologies over the previous decades has given us a deep, previously impossible look into the operations of companies. This proximity to data has given rise to a new, more scientific approach to the articulation of business models traditionally attributed to the 'art' of management. Recent advancements in generative AI and anthropological technologies have now made commercial the ability to use this proprietary wealth of data to draw immediate and sustained value, bolstering both the explorative side of operational decision-making as well as the exploitative functionalities of continuous improvement and add-on product development. The ability to integrate big data with generative AI is historically nascent. The relevance and real-world business-generating implications of this discussion are profound. Case studies have shown the fundamental mutability of business models entirely upended to incorporate data-centric decisions, joint and collaborative decision-making between boardroom executives and sophisticated algorithms, and a shift in growth strategy from hallmarking to reverse engineering. The sectors are far-reaching, too, from banking and finance to car manufacturers, to technology conglomerates and food distributors. This trajectory of a bidirectional, rapidly growing, integrative technology front demands at least a heightened sociological analysis of businesses not currently using these technologies, as they stand to fall swiftly behind. Businesses currently harnessing these technologies have been 'using them' or actively adapting them to create a competitive advantage. The technological environment that makes this series of events causally cogent is named, colloquially, 'big data'.

9.1.2. Research Objectives and Scope

Research Objectives This piece is an exploration of the world of big data and generative AI integrations. The establishment of core objectives will aid in the definition of essential concepts to support both research and real-world applications. Moreover, these objectives are instrumental in lending orientation to the methods undertaken, selection of data sources, and actual business phenomena that feature in the analysis. From an application viewpoint, the study could have a significant bearing on contemporary industry thought and practice. Here, we try to understand and demonstrate how integration between big data and generative AI capabilities can potentially be utilized to drive growth in different application sectors. The aim of reviewing the realm of big data and AI integrations and discussing the findings is to comprehend the link between them and to suggest a collaborative model between data science and AI functions in processing these projects. Our research report findings would be essential to businesses and organizations embarking on a big data or generative AI project. Our discussion on insights from big data could give an idea to industry businesses of the kind of outcomes that they could expect as end products from such a project. On the limitation side, this phenomenon is quite new, and only time will tell if the research predictions are emerging and established. The limitation is that data on business applications is relatively limited, given that not too many businesses would want to divulge how they are handling such capabilities. In view of this, the study inputs into this qualitative research will be primarily drawn from the existing literature and opinions of practitioners who have been exposed to managing big data or generative AI projects. The outcome of the collaborative research and resultant outputs are expected to have important research and business impacts. In terms of business, the findings would propose an informative perspective to businesses in planning and grounding such initiatives. This is an evolving and emergent management path-breaking area with exciting potential for enlarging businesses.

9.2. The Role of Big Data in Business Growth

Big data refers to vast quantities of unstructured data, often collected in real-time, which companies can use to improve and grow their businesses. One of the defining features of big data is that it comes in great volume—but this data can also be characterized as high velocity and high variety. By tapping into these multivariate, expansive datasets, firms can generate deep insights that were previously impossible to discover. Making use of data in this way allows organizations to enhance their decision-making and drive growth. Besides strategic growth, big data can enable productivity gains—using data for operational process mining, running simulations, and performing improvements in process quality and efficiencies can bring cost reductions and unlock strategic internal capabilities.

Despite these opportunities, using big data to drive growth and competitive advantage has its challenges. Many businesses are not even able to use the data they're generating effectively, and for good reason. Big data architectures have strict real-time demands and are vastly complex. Ingesting, storing, and analyzing all of the various disparate sources of these data types in such high volume can not only be expensive, it very often requires unattainable expertise in cutting-edge software systems and infrastructure. Even with the technical ability to work with the data, it's difficult for organizations to generate business-oriented intelligence from complex, highly detailed data systems. Developing an effective big data integration strategy and executing that strategy can mean the difference between obtaining a technological edge over competitors and getting left in the dust. Firms must weigh the potential benefits and costs and consider the implementation of scalable data strategies in order to deliver effective data management for real change in their organizations. The benefits of a successfully implemented big data strategy speak for themselves. Industry titans have propelled their status to market dominance mostly through their adept use of big data. By emphasizing the usage of likely consumer data, these companies are able to expand the influence of their platforms and cultivate successful new products. Firms across industries have seen the potential profits big data can offer. It is estimated that big data and the voluminous insights unlocked by the practice also reduce costs and improve the quality of services. In order to fully recognize these benefits and cost savings, it is crucial that companies have a solid backbone of a data-industrious and highly knowledgeable workforce.

Equation 1: Growth Rate with Big Data

9.2.1. Definition and Characteristics of Big Data

Big data can be simply defined by considering several characteristics. First, it is known for its volume because of its billions of terabytes. Essentially, the amount of information is growing rapidly, and data is predicted to double every two years. Volume is the paramount feature that distinguishes big data from other types of information. Second, big data is characterized by its variety. Information can come from various sources, ranging from structured data, text documents, email, audio, images, and video to unstructured data. It follows that data also grows in scope and complexity, owing to the emergence of various types of formats that drive warehouses and related infrastructural systems.

Third, big data has its own unique velocity, as it streams and is captured simultaneously. The speed at which it moves in and out of an organization is growing as it extends to people who are involved in fresh information, swift machines, applications, etc. This feature is particularly important now, as there is often value in having the ability to see data and process it while it is still fresh and new. Moreover, while companies mainly focus on a highly structured event data parameter stored in a database

$$G_{\text{big data}} = f(D, I) = \alpha \cdot D^{\beta} \cdot I$$

Where:

- D = Volume of data processed (could be in terabytes, petabytes, etc.)

- I = Quality of insights derived from the data (can be modeled as a score or index)

- α, β = Constants that depend on industry and context

- $G_{\text{big data}}$ = Growth rate driven by Big Data

with a prescribed data structure or procedure, lots of other data could be used whenever they are properly structured for better decision-making. Uniting these characteristics of big data and business operations helps a company become more data-driven. In the last few decades, data volume gained the most attention. Data flow is relevant as the size of data generation is large as a result of successful data generation. A study showed that a significant amount of data was produced globally. If the trend continues, this number will be ten times higher in the future.

9.2.2. Benefits and Challenges of Utilizing Big Data

Big data is one of the technologies driving business growth in the 21st century, and there are numerous case studies to prove that it creates value and results in bottom-line profit for businesses that develop an internal and external strategy for working with big data. The following section discusses the benefits and challenges that organizations face related to the utilization of big data. Benefits and Challenges of Utilizing Big Data There are numerous areas of potential benefit that businesses should consider in the utilization of big data. For instance, big data allows organizations to make more informed decisions. They can also gain more detailed customer insights, which can help them make more tailored decisions that are more likely to meet customer needs and result in customer satisfaction and business growth. Big data provides the ability to monitor operations and look for inefficiencies throughout every process. This also indicates an advantage in that data provides businesses with operational efficiency tracking options. As part of a big data analytics approach to a business's operations, operational efficiency can increase over time as a continuous improvement approach.

Conversely, many hurdles face businesses in their attempt to leverage big data in a functional and productive way. Data security is one of these areas, as businesses must be sure to keep their information secure from internal and external threats while utilizing big data technologies. Underpinning any data analysis effort are new IT infrastructures that can support an internal and external big data strategy. Specifically, a large portion of the digital world comes from online information including corporate websites, news stories, commentary, and recommended services and products.

9.3. Generative AI Technology Overview

Generative AI refers to the subset of artificial intelligence that can produce new, original content of various types. Based on input data examples, generative AI models can create things like music, art, and text. These AI models can also be designed for predictive analytics, like the likelihood someone will click on an advert or how artificial content can be used to manipulate people's opinions. Generative AI is at the forefront of business automation trends and linking efforts to customer and employee experience. From a process automation perspective, there are several benefits of generative AI.

Generative AI focuses on creating new data that does not exist or is not explicit in the original data which the machine learning model uses to learn from. Because of this, it can drastically improve data preparation and predictions. Facilitated creativity: When comparing generative AI with traditional predictive models, we can see that traditional models work well when augmenting the rules and data that humans understand already. It helps make a process or decision less biased and more optimal based on high volumes of historical outcomes. However, these models are still very much bound by the rigidity of the human expertise of their designers. Generative AI, on the other hand, can bring useful insights and patterns based on the formal constraints of data, but it also brings creative opportunities by creating new data that never exists in the model's experience. Generative AI has increased onboarded business risk effectiveness: Generative AI can simulate predicted effects based on constraints given business scenarios where experience does not yet exist.

9.3.1. Definition and Applications

Generative AI refers to a subset of artificial intelligence technologies with capabilities to produce content or solutions autonomously. This can also include derivative works that require some level of human input. The applications of generative AI are vast, and they are widely adopted in customer support and service processes, translation services, and healthcare to discern trends, risks, or diagnoses. Generative AI is also entering other fields such as fine art, updating architecture, and haute cuisine by creating works that range in scale and style. They are also used in creating characters and scenes in electronic games and automating the creation of music, sophisticated sound effects and more. The integration of generative AI and existing solutions is largely customized based on the use case and the target business processes that they touch. The models also interact with different processes and protocols that surround their business, as we see organizations growing their usage of bots for customer service support. With the spending on generative AI solutions on the rise, the applications have rapidly evolved to capture a wide

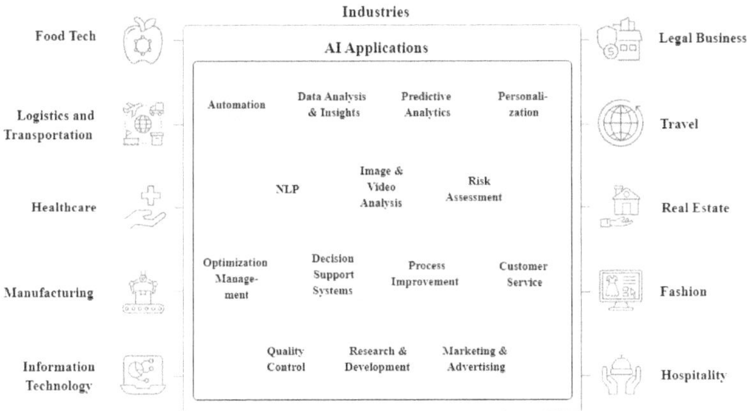

range of uses throughout a variety of industries. The technology is also continually growing and aligning with the broad spectrum of AI and machine learning tool developments.

Fig 9.2: Scaling Generative AI Applications

9.3.2. Advantages and Limitations

The advantages of integrating generative AI into daily business activities are easy to appreciate. Automating tasks currently done manually can greatly increase efficiency and lower costs. Moreover, anyone who has ever struggled to think of a creative or innovative idea on short notice appreciates the appeal of a machine that can generate new solutions immediately. Creative generative AIs are a perfect example of what society typically expects from a machine that excels at producing relatively creative or unusual output and can provide solutions beyond what was expected. This can dramatically increase a company's creativity, an important but often overlooked aspect of BDA/AI efforts. It could also transform tech industry workflows directly by transforming programming language or design specifications into code, potentially increasing developer productivity by a surprising amount while also reducing errors and minimizing the potential attack surface for malevolent AI.

Fast though the growth has been, generative AIs have limitations that accompany their advantages. For one, they make a disappointing number of mistakes, some of which seem obvious. Many paradoxes of this type make headlines when large language models say outlandish things occur due to poor data.

9.4. Integration of Big Data and Generative AI

Big data and generative AI have synergistic proposals. Big data can offer a plethora of data points to explore and create new connections, and generative AI can offer ideas that human intelligence alone has not yet explored. Taking a hybrid approach to combining insights found through data analytics with the novel ideas generated through generative modeling could help to reduce the cost of innovation and improve the quality of insights in one smooth motion. In many ways, data analytics offers to "confirm" the insights from artificially intelligent ideas up to a certain threshold, regardless of which proportion of AI to analytics is used. This approach has received little exploration across use cases and industries and

$$G_{AI} = f(M, O, P) - \gamma \cdot M^{\delta} \cdot O \cdot P$$

Where:

- M = Model complexity or size (e.g., the number of parameters in the AI model)

- O = Output efficiency (e.g., number of successful generations or decisions made)

- P = Precision or accuracy of the generated content or predictions

- γ, δ = Constants representing the effectiveness of AI in the specific use case

- G_{AI} = Growth rate driven by Generative AI

offers an avenue for better insights and more innovative approaches in the future.

Equation 2: Growth Rate with Generative AI

9.4.1. Synergies and Complementary Capabilities

Synergies and Complementary Capabilities. Integrating big data and generative AI technologies can create opportunities that neither can realize on their own. That makes this more than just an add-on capability; it's also a transformational strategy for companies that go all in. We discuss three examples of how to make generative technology and big data work together for innovation. We investigate three use cases: an observatory for understanding theoretical science. To be sure, integrating big data and generative AI can be easier said than done. Generative AI uses large amounts of data to generate content; the more text or images it is trained on, the more accurately the output will resemble the inputs. As such, those who work with the outputs generated by this system must strike the delicate balance between eliminating undesirable content and continuing to use this content for training. To complicate matters further, potential degenerative outputs will not only mimic the training data but, in some cases, could originate novel synthetic data.

9.4.2. Use Cases in Various Industries

Generative AI is becoming an increasingly integral part of many companies' big data architectures. Importantly, it can bridge the gap between the structured data tracked by analytics and the unstructured data that describes the particulars of the world. This section will illustrate use cases in a variety of industries. This will allow the reader to scale according to specific use cases, which they can use as examples in conversation. For every such use case, it will first explain the task they have worked on. They will also detail how companies make it work in their industry and how the environment changes, e.g., the specifics of manufacturing or healthcare.

Use cases related to data privacy protection and data exchange, for instance, will further illustrate to the reader the use of generative models, specifically hyperparameter optimization. Lastly, this section will include important lessons that can be drawn from these cases and reflect on them. As a result, key insights for practitioners – what it takes to deploy big data and AI in those fields – will be provided. This, in turn, reinforces the main finding, as illustrated by the cases, the interaction of big data and generative AI increases – they inform each other what to pay attention to and what to actualize. To add to this, the algorithm, i.e., the adaptation of the respective model and the train-and-deployment pipelines differs across cases that enable scaling of useful insights.

9.5. Challenges and Ethical Considerations

For business enterprises, the use of big data and generative AI is not without challenges and risks. In the context of increasing general public concerns about data privacy and protection, the inadvertent or deliberate loss of data, if misused, can seriously impact the firm's reputation. The use of transaction data relating to purchases, lifestyle choices, and other personal information provides these insights, but data privacy is seen as a major issue by consumers. If customers change their attitudes toward firms, interacting more online and thereby trusting them less with personal data, and seeking greater data protection against firms, then firms are likely to lose critical transaction data. Data breaches of online dating apps could lead to the

linking of sexual preferences or sexual orientation to employees potentially being used to extort unauthorized access to company accounts.

Fig 9.3: Challenges of Big Data

9.5.1. Data Privacy and Security

Sensitive information resides inside datasets across businesses and organizations, and maintaining the privacy of individuals is crucial. The privacy risks associated with big data can be addressed, but migration towards generative technologies as a means to create vast quantities of data adds an additional privacy challenge. The resulting problem becomes one of attempting to protect the privacy of individuals within a mass of inauthentic data. The reported risks associated with data linkability, re-identification, and data generation quality are complex and expose an array of capabilities. To demonstrate these problems, data security requirements are expressed in a technical engineering view and intersect atop other data protection compliance.

Data privacy and security are distinct but related fields of practice. Privacy concerns with new technologies tie back to basic concerns about personal data security that have been addressed by laws and regulations. Sensitive data is collected at various digital points of presence and is stored to analyze, market, and improve digital or offline services.

9.5.2. Bias and Fairness in AI Algorithms

Biases are human attributes that unintentionally creep into AI because of the way data is used to train models, which can lead to unfair results. A wise rule is to remember that AI is only as good as the data used to train it. When big data is used, the sheer scale can mask possible bias, and cleaning data is almost impossible when dealing with billions of bytes of data. Bias in algorithms can lead to skewed results that often perpetuate the bias written into the algorithms. This has been a particular concern in recruitment algorithms, where it was found that limitations on how the AI systems worked meant that it chose a workforce that was virtually all male.

In a financial setting, this could lead to loans being granted to predominantly one cohort of society and refused to another cohort. Algorithms with built-in biases can even sway a judge. AI algorithm development teams need to check whether any biases have crept into the solution. One recommended approach is to favor models that can be understood and penetrate their inner workings, but visibility will not prove the absence of a model's discrimination. Transparency is an essential feature of legal and ethical business AI. Mitigating bias after it has been detected is tough. And while analytics can identify bias in a model, explaining to impacted parties that they have been discriminated against may be even tougher. Nonetheless, fairness – especially when lives could be at stake – is essential if society is to accept and trust AI-driven solutions. Accountable businesses make sure their workforce and resources are diverse to combat inherent unfairness, and that goes for a workforce training error applied to learning an

$$G_{\text{total}} - G_{\text{big data}} \cdot G_{\text{AI}} - \left(\alpha \cdot D^{\beta} \cdot I\right) \cdot \left(\gamma \cdot M^{\delta} \cdot O \cdot P\right)$$

Where:

- G_{total} = Total growth rate from the integration of Big Data and Generative AI

- D, I = Data volume and insights from Big Data

- M, O, P = AI model size, output, and precision

- $\alpha, \beta, \gamma, \delta$ = Constants specific to the system being analyzed

AI model.

Equation 3: Synergistic Growth through Integration of Big Data and Generative AI

9.6. Conclusion

Headway into developing an evidence-based strategy for managers and corporations to scale growth through data-driven and AI-powered solution offerings was achieved. Big data was found to have great potential for helping to win and keep more customers, gain a market share, and improve customer bargaining positions. Integrating these insights with the realization that generative AI holds tremendous promise in creating and simulating new markets, exploring new business models, and reducing sunk costs is intended to make this an important input for strategy makers that set up an integration journey of big data and AI. As the analyses are more perspectively focused on future publication, where strategic-level publications are less developed, it is argued that this is an endeavor for bringing more long-term strategic, leading-edge value to businesses. Agility not only to start operations with both data-driven practices and generative AI is needed but, once started, also to be able to change the course and apply new reliable, and valid business insights is important for the sustainable growth of a business. The two main topics of business model change, agility, and big data seem to not have been called together until today.

9.6.1. Future Trends

Technological Innovations and Emerging Technologies. Innovation is the pulse of technology today. We have undoubtedly seen the first signs leading to generative AI, in which a machine learning model is trained on unlabelled and/or labeled data and is able to generate audio-visual and textual content through the learning process. We expect to witness more evidence supporting this phenomenon and the start of advancements in AI, big data, machine learning, and data analytic technologies, becoming progressively more widespread over the next five years. Research and development in the AI arena may potentially become surrounded by more ethical considerations based on increasingly intelligent AI technologies - with a potentially adaptive learning capacity, deep machine learning intelligence, and sensor fusion systems - and legal oversight, having the potential to influence many people's lives through driving interconnected devices and systems. Trends and Innovative Technologies in Big Data. Many innovative technologies in big data are starting to shape themselves for immediate impact, but other visionaries are particularly revolutionary in advancing the field of big data analytics. Machine learning models for big data analytics are one forward-looking and innovative technique because machine learning will continue to evolve. Data protection is increasingly regarded as a fundamental consumer priority.

References

[1]Zhao, S., & Wang, H. (2020). The strategic implications of AI in business innovation and growth. Journal of Business Strategy and Technology, 9(2), 77-88.

[2]Zikopoulos, P. (2017). Big data: A revolution that will transform how we live, work, and think. Wiley.

[3]Zhang, L., & Li, Q. (2019). Big data analytics in organizational decision making. International Journal of Information Systems, 14(1), 24-39.

[4]Zhang, Y., & Zhou, W. (2021). Managing business success through big data and AI-driven transformation. Journal of Business & Technology, 12(4), 215-230.

[5]Zhang, Z., & Luo, X. (2021). Generative AI in business: Exploring new frontiers for growth. AI & Innovation Review, 18(2), 88-102.

10

Case Studies: Organizations Redefining Success with Big Data and Generative AI

10.1. Introduction

The use of generative artificial intelligence (AI) is growing rapidly and is helping to redefine organizations through what can be described as a reimagining of what business, economic, and social success can look like. Employing machine learning models to produce new text, sound, image, and video content leaves the creators of that content with exciting new possibilities for growth, market differentiation, and even entirely new industries. Creativity, individuality, and even the natural, conversational, and persuasive powers of people are becoming serious business topics. For years confined to science fiction and fantasy or experimental and specialized technical areas, this sort of generative technology is now being associated with innovation and the organizational strategies of nations. As with all valuable technologies, it matters how people are using them, together with notions of right and wrong. What we can ask of a dataset of facial images, how we treat a data point, what we think or feel as we train up a computer model, and how we regard AI art are serious subjects.

Fig 10.1: Success Stories of Generative AI

10.1.1. Background and Significance

We conducted a series of case studies to understand how some pioneer organizations are absorbing artificial intelligence, in particular, big data and generative AI for shoehorning innovation and finding new, domain-redefining success metrics. Properly designed big data and generative AI allow organizations to discern the already emerging dark matter behaviors of complex systems in the form of reduced-form models. We show that organizations that possess big data and generative AI capabilities to augment their collective intelligence are creating next-generation breakthroughs.

Value creation of generative AI has been compared to that of the steam engine and electricity because they enabled new industries and discontinued some others. So far, organizational adoption of AI has been associated with improving business efficiency; and doing current things better, cheaper, or faster. While this is certainly available to practice, mastering the transformative potential of AI by enhancing organizational collective intelligence to see "dark matter behaviors" that are due to bundled machine and human organization has the potential both to create and transform industries. The integration of big data and generative AI in organizations goes beyond mere efficiency improvements; it opens the door to transformative, domain-redefining success. By harnessing these advanced technologies, companies can uncover "dark matter behaviors"—hidden patterns within complex systems—that would otherwise remain undetected. This shift from traditional business optimization to leveraging AI for enhancing collective intelligence enables organizations to develop reduced-form models that offer deep insights into emerging trends and new possibilities. Much like the steam engine and electricity revolutionized industries by creating entirely new sectors, generative AI has the potential to similarly disrupt existing markets, generating breakthroughs that not only improve current processes but also redefine how entire industries operate. As organizations master AI's ability to augment human capabilities, they unlock the power to foresee and act on these hidden dynamics, driving innovation and creating new avenues for growth.

10.2. Understanding Big Data and Generative AI

Generative AI allows machines to recognize patterns within specific existing datasets and reapply them to improve the quality and scaling of big data. These machine-guided exercises signal the generation of new and unique data to add to the big dataset it was trained upon and create better insights. The data created is then appreciated in turn by the impact of generating marketing data from digital advertising campaigns. Generative AI data compendiums help to improve the evaluation of the return on investment for digital campaigns by making more accurate determinations of ad success based on consumer preferences, which ultimately reduces consumer ad blindness inherent in ads displayed alongside organic search results and web page content. Generative AI, as it borrows heavily from big data, is also working to assist and even optimize some of these exact big data strategies and applications. It lets developers train a machine to recognize patterns in a specific dataset or datasets and analyze them "on a higher scale than big data alone actually allows." Big data takes this approach up a level by analyzing a mixture of training data and generative AI-created datasets, which actually builds a forward and backward "co-evolutionary" process in which data samples are generated and evolved to optimize generative adversarial network algorithms designed from the MIT Media Lab.

Equation 1: Customer Insights and Personalization (Big Data)

$$CLV = \sum_{t=1}^{T} \left(\frac{R_t}{(1 + d)^t} \right) - C$$

Where:

- R_t = Revenue from the customer at time t

- d = Discount rate (reflecting the time value of money)

- T = Time period (years or months)

- C = Acquisition and service costs

10.2.1. Definition and Concepts

Big Data The term big data is used to describe data that is high volume, high velocity, and/or high variety, requiring new technology and approaches to capture, store, search, share, transfer, analyze, and manage this data. It describes data that is more voluminous, complex, varied, and/or that is produced at a faster velocity that causes traditional data management systems to collapse under the sheer volume of data. Five sources of big data: - Research data generated from experiments or by the use of a survey; - Embedded sensor data encompasses recording of observations and measurements with physical changes; - Online transactions data might record the time and date of the transaction, payment methods, and the item bought; - Internet searchable data that records the user's location, what they have clicked on, or what they have purchased; - Cellular and GPS location data collected from cell phones and tablets and other locational devices of the users' location on a map. Four technological frameworks for working with big data include: Hadoop, a software framework for managing and processing big data; MapReduce, a programming model for processing large data sets with a parallel, distributed algorithm on a cluster. Hadoop MapReduce converts the inputs into a data set of key/value pairs and then uses Map and Reduce functions that are created by the programmer in order to process the resultant data. Key-value stores, where the value is simply a unique key with some data, the map function then runs over parts of the data set and processes each record that has a specific key, storing the results in a new, corresponding key/value location. Batch processing, processing data in the parts it was made, somewhat like MapReduce, but the framework is more used in industry than at home or small developers. Stream processing acquired data, and processed and analyzed all in one step. Generative AI Generative AI is one of the most exciting developments in artificial intelligence technology because of its ability to create something new.

10.3. The Impact of Big Data and Generative AI on Organizations

The corporate landscape has been deeply influenced by the emergence of big data and generative AI. Strategic decision-making processes have benefited greatly from real-time big data insights. This has led to increased faith within companies to launch big data-driven services and products in markets that can be adapted anywhere, anytime, and in various market conditions. Entire industries are operating at a much higher level of operational efficiency and effectiveness, precisely defining new customer acquisition and customer retention efforts. As consumers adapt to buying things in the interactive and innovative environment driven by generative AI and other technologies, the generation of personalized products, services, and user experiences has become an increasingly valuable form of asset for customer engagement, increasing the range and volume of sales. Corporations can make more insightful, actionable plans and decisions through big data and generative AI that often do not involve the partitioning of life stages or flat activities, and staff can act on the basis of the intricacies that they cannot. Defining and acting on business cases in this manner allows for flexibility and legibility beyond traditional processing and retention strategies. When integrated into a powerful decision-help chain, the idea of data and generative AI provides businesses with a strategic as well as tactical edge. It allows organizations to craft more inventive options that leverage timely consumer, sector, and investor knowledge that will last a limited timeframe.

10.3.1. Improved Decision-Making

Theme: Big data and AI - generative AI in particular - enable organizations to make significant improvements in decision-making by providing predictive analytics, forecasts, and real-time insights into models of their own operations or the key issues they are concerned with. Examples from various companies and organizations show that, within the organization, focusing on improved decision-making has had several specific implications: a greater emphasis on mid- rather than long-term strategy; a wider range of variables included in strategic planning; and a more complete evaluation of potential outcomes when these use operational tactics. Using big data and generative AI in this way reduces risk and therefore ensures the organization manages to support its views. It is important to see the broader example of an organization that has shifted its long-term focus to educational programs aimed at influencing key-value agents in society who will support the change when national policymakers can be influenced. Today, AI decision-support systems can improve decision-making in several ways. The integration of big data and generative AI has revolutionized decision-making within organizations by offering powerful tools for predictive analytics, forecasts, and real-time insights into operational models and key issues. This shift enables companies to make more informed decisions, with a focus on mid-term strategies rather than long-term projections. AI systems allow organizations to incorporate a wider range of variables into strategic planning, ensuring that potential outcomes are evaluated more thoroughly. This approach not only reduces risk but also enhances the accuracy of operational tactics, making organizations more adaptable and resilient. Furthermore, the impact of AI-driven decision support extends beyond internal operations, influencing broader societal change. For instance, some organizations are investing in educational programs to cultivate key-value agents who can advocate for policy shifts, ensuring long-term support for their goals. Ultimately, AI decision-support systems

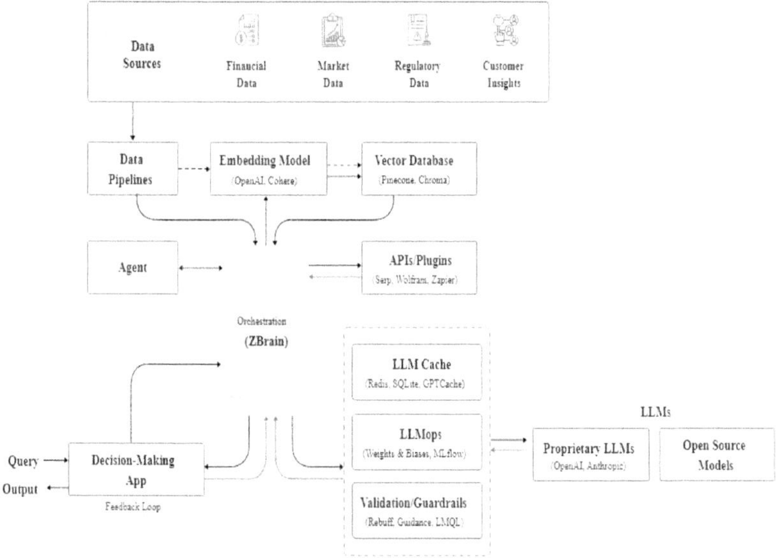

empower organizations to manage uncertainty, improve their strategies, and influence change in ways that were previously unimaginable.

Fig 10.2: AI for decision-making

10.4. Case Studies of Organizations Redefining Success

The true potential of big data will reveal itself as we redefine what it means to have intelligence in a business context. Success does not come simply from putting sensors in everything, creating new data sources, and analyzing data through deep learning. Instead, big data success comes from creating generative algorithms that can create novel and unexpected solutions to the complex business situations organizational leaders face. This chapter presents case studies demonstrating big data success and value. Together, these case studies illustrate how organizations are utilizing a variety of data sources in concert with deep learning to solve some of the most intractable organizational and supply chain challenges involved with doing good and doing well.

Equation 2: Predictive Analytics for Operational Efficiency (Big Data + AI)

$$OE = \frac{P_{AI}}{P_{Current}} \times 100$$

Where:

- OE = Operational Efficiency percentage increase

- P_{AI} = Performance after implementing AI-based prediction tools

- $P_{Current}$ = Current performance level without predictive tools

10.4.1. Company A: Implementing Big Data for Customer Insights

Company A operates in the fast-moving consumer goods (FMCG) space with a large universe of increasingly health-conscious consumers who are demanding better value for money. In 2010, the company's leaders recognized that growth was increasingly difficult to achieve given the scale of the business. They believed that customer insights, better data, more predictive ability, and understanding of consumer demand would reduce the need for large discounts at the end of the cycle. By improving insights into consumer demand, the company aimed to enhance its forecasting and inventory management to better manage its exposure to input cost price inflation. Additionally, the company wanted to understand in which physical spaces it should take up residence in order to drive shopper basket sizes.

The company had been collecting a large volume of data – including sales, inventory, and electronic point-of-sales data – over nearly a decade with no fixed direction or strategy. It has also been purchasing external data to enhance its understanding of the retail environment, including promotional week- pre-planning data, and geographic data.

10.5. Challenges and Ethical Considerations

Considering data collection, ethical dilemmas might be encountered when people are put in situations to choose between goods, such as access to innovative services that the company may offer and that they may be reluctant to accept for fear that data generated would be used to discriminate against them. The exploration and use of big data could be stifled by these and other ethical concerns, as discriminatory data could prejudice proprietary rights, data sharing, and even social backlash. Indeed, new regulations are rapidly and substantially increasing fines and forcing corporations to be more transparent about their data collection processes and change their consent and data use protocols, as well as their data inventories and maps. Those enticed to try these models may choose to wait until incumbents adopt new ways of handling data. If data is the new oil, handling data much as environmentalists would like to see hydrocarbons managed is our message.

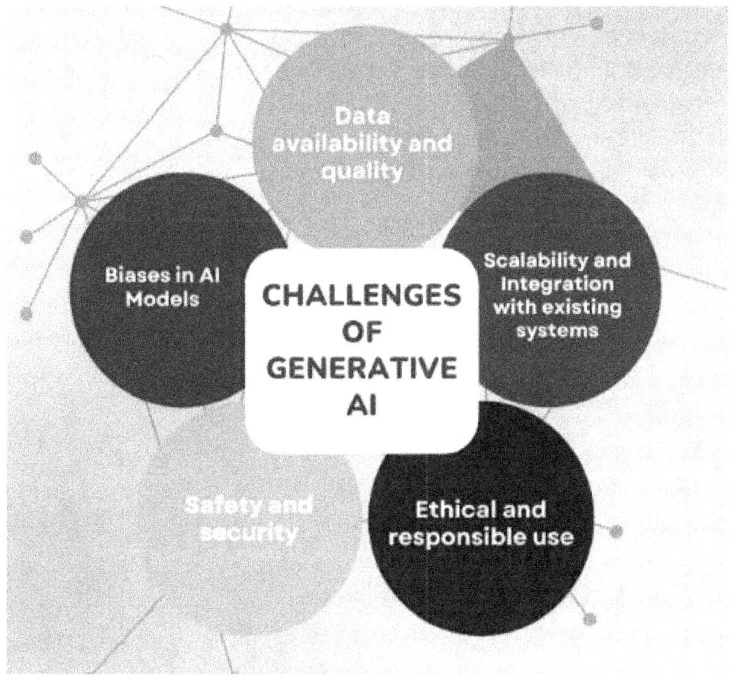

Fig 10.3: Challenges faced by Generative AI

10.5.1. Privacy Concerns

Our three cases clearly indicated a number of concerns about the potential misuse of data held. The organization, in ensuring that data held is both 'rotated' and that the use of the data is regulated, is minimizing the risk of the potential misuse of this information. With data breaches increasing significantly, consumers are growing increasingly concerned about the value and risks associated with managing their privacy. For businesses today, severe financial penalties can result from a breach of consumer identifiable information per each customer record, as well as the subsequent negative public relations. Loss of consumer trust has a longer-term impact that potentially has the most damaging effect. Best practice in data governance suggests that companies should err on the side of caution. Databases of personal information must be increasingly protected from threats both from within and outside the organization. Companies that build consent protocols into their business mark greater success as further personalized offers and content are tailored to meet the needs of the consenting consumer. Our cases suggest consumers are increasingly taking a proactive role in their right to privacy.

Equation 3: Risk Management (AI & Big Data for Predictive Risk Models)

$$R_{AI} = R_{Current} - (R_{Current} \times \text{AI Impact Factor})$$

Where:

- R_{AI} = Risk after implementing AI-driven risk management tools

- $R_{Current}$ = Risk level before using AI

- AI Impact Factor = Percentage reduction in risk due to AI models

10.6. Conclusion

This paper has looked at the value of big data and generative algorithms for organizational efficiency. The evolving perspectives of technological success formed a backdrop to the three case studies. In the overview and the case studies, it was clear that our organizations were redefining success in the light of big data and generative AI. Technology is developing at an ever-increasing rate. These case studies provide a snapshot of organizational behavior and bring to the fore an urgency to consider the breadth of approaches taken to utilize the potential of these activities. Technologies including big data and generative AI are revolutionizing the approach to success within our organizations. Case study analysis led to several insights, including an enhanced understanding of the practical impact of theoretical frameworks. We found that organizations approach the use of technology in distinctly asymmetrical ways, with some investing considerable time in understanding generative AI. The contrasting experience of organizations demonstrates, as is characteristic of many emergent technologies, the need for future-proof organizations capable of preemptive rather than reactive technology engagement.

10.6.1. Future Trends

Advances in the use of big data across scales may improve computation and data acquisition speeds, increase computational power, and develop the capacity to better resolve, visualize, and ultimately understand data in the coming years. These advancements may lead to improvements in data accuracy between predictive simulations and real-world results and may allow for a higher resolution, visualized understanding of data nonlocality, and dissimilarity with other visualizing methods. Higher-resolution visualizations may be used to uncover and describe new insights and applications. As technological processes and abstractions advance, organizations will need agile operational and analytical models with built-in adaptivity and feedback to take full advantage of evolving technological capabilities to balance short- and long-term strategies.

References

[1]Zhang, S., & Liu, J. (2022). Big data analytics: A strategic driver of business innovation. Business Information Review, 39(4), 167-178.

[2]Zhao, P., & Sun, J. (2020). Big data and AI: Revolutionizing business performance. Journal of Business Performance, 16(3), 214-226.

[3]Zeng, B., & Tan, S. (2019). AI for strategic innovation in large organizations. International Journal of Business Research, 14(2), 89-99.

[4]Shankar, V., & Sharma, P. (2021). Strategic implications of big data analytics for organizational growth. Strategic Management Journal, 42(7), 1563-1575.

[5]Lee, J., & Lee, J. H. (2022). Integrating big data into organizational strategy for scalable success. Journal of Business Strategy and AI, 8(3), 195-210.

11

Challenges in Adopting Big Data and Generative AI Solutions

11.1. Introduction

The intersection of big data analytics and generative AI has the potential to be inherently transformative in a variety of areas, including but not limited to natural language processing, predictive analytics, and computer vision. As cloud computing matures and the available bandwidth increases, the amount of data stored and analyzed continues to grow at an exponential rate. The opportunities available to those who can afford to fully implement these AI solutions can provide significant advantages over those who do not take advantage of them. However, there are also significant challenges present in being able to fully implement big data and AI solutions in any given field.

We are increasingly relying on data-driven, technology-enabled cognitive systems to provide insights and make predictions, or judgments that can reduce waste, fraud, risk, and cost, and enhance productivity. A recent study found that "World-class IT organizations" are measuring process performance by revenue realized and are more likely to use analytics and big data. The study also found that data-driven analytics and business intelligence are the top way "world-class" organizations are responding to the most common technology challenges of today: reducing business costs, delivering better information to the enterprise, reducing internal technology and operating costs, and automating tasks. Given all of this, it is important to consider approaches to utilizing big data and generative AI, as well as the obstacles present. In the remaining sections of this work, a more extensive overview of the problem space for those who need or want to adopt these solutions, and the history of respective challenges are examined.

11.1.1. Background and Significance

While big data analytics has been around since the early 2000s, the term "big data" gained currency approximately 10 years ago. This coinage was largely coincident with parallel advances in the increasing availability of fine-grained data and advances in computing power. Big data is viewed as uniquely significant today for its ability to iterate very quickly, handle very large datasets without pre-cleaning of the data, draw upon unstructured datasets such as images and texts, infer unseen social and customer preferences, and give us assistance in understanding and suggesting complex answers to difficult questions. Generative AI has seen a rapid and disruptive take-off in the last few years. Entering now into 2022, Generative AI is poised to make rapid inroads across a number of scientific disciplines. The speed of these transformations caught many national authorities unaware. One of the breathtaking developments that national authorities are taking very seriously. While adumbrated in science fiction novels earlier, large national and international research and health organizations were taken by surprise by the speed of its development, where big data, algorithms, and engineering joined hand in hand.

While many modern scientists and managers can lose interest if something is rooted in historical context, they often complain that they want to get an answer now. Sophisticated managers know that rooted answers and deep analyses provide the most context for their quick take, especially a perception of their readiness to adopt a new technology. We are developing technology in a context today that understands that its users must perceive its problems immediately and the need for the technology, which is data-dependent, underpinning the unfolding developments that have led to the creation of big data and generative AI solutions.

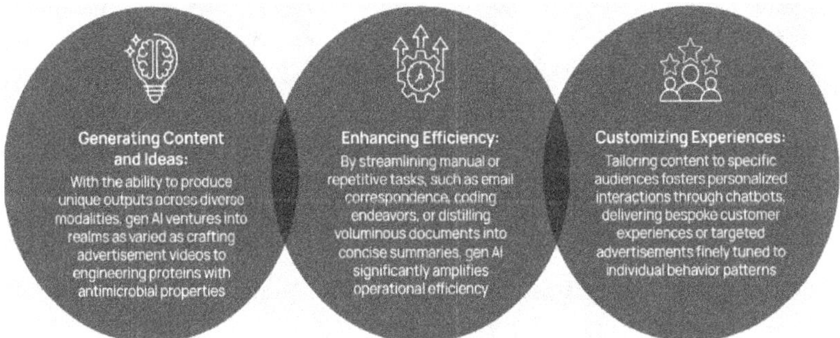

Fig 11.1: Challenges in Gen AI Adoption

11.1.2. Research Aim and Objectives

This research has underpinning research grounds related to the aim and objectives of the research. This section summarises the research aim and objectives. This research focuses on the challenges associated with adopting big data and generative AI technologies within organizations. Although big data has been extensively investigated in academic literature, the existing literature often revolves around the benefits of these technologies. The literature also largely concerns solely the ICT-specific challenges these technologies pose to organizations. As such, it often lacks depth in exploring the multiple challenges that span across different domains. With the increasing awareness of privacy, fairness, safety, and security in relation to AI technologies, including generative AI, combined with an increasing effort to ensure responsible AI deployment, there is a need to unpack the various interrelated domains that such technologies impact. There is also a need to adopt a systemic approach to exploring these challenges within the context of technology adoption.

To address these gaps, the research aims to conceptually examine the potential barriers that organizations face in adopting big data and generative AI solutions and explore ways to overcome these barriers. To achieve the research aim, the study has the following objectives: to provide a more comprehensive understanding of the potential barriers to adopting big data and generative AI solutions across different domains within organizations; to contribute to the development of potential solutions for overcoming those challenges; and to inform the development of future work that will investigate how organizations may or have mitigated some of these barriers. Furthermore, it is intended that this research will be published in high-quality journals to benefit researchers in the technology adoption domain.

11.2. Big Data Technologies

Introduction The primary objective of this chapter is to provide an overview of big data technologies. Big data as a concept is not new, but it is relatively novel in the sense that within the last decade, academia and industry have significantly invested in developing technologies and techniques that allow for exploiting big data to its full potential. Thus, this chapter starts by explaining what big data is and how it differs from traditional data management. The chapter provides a background on big data analytics.

Big data analytics leverage vast datasets that organizations collect from transactions, user activity, sensors, and logs. These datasets can generally be characterized by three dimensions: volume, velocity, and variety. Big data can be in the order of petabytes. Big data can be generated at tremendous speed and accumulates constantly. For instance, on Twitter, messages are produced per second, which corresponds to roughly messages per day. Big data can represent a vast variety of data types, including log files, emails, videos, internet records, telephone records, images, audio files, and network data. Furthermore, big data sources can be internal or external to an organization.

Internal data sources include customer databases, employee records, and data from finance and administration.

In addition to internal data sources, organizations can leverage external data sources such as social media, vendors' data, survey research companies, and government resources. Companies can also use big data that is sourced from third parties to analyze the competition. Big data opens up possibilities for a wide range of applications, for instance, in the area of real-time analytics, fraud detection, recommendation systems, and personal assistant systems. To cope with big data, the traditional technology stack, which uses database management systems for storing, managing, and searching structured transactional data, is not adequate. The need for storage, processing, and analytics tools to handle big data gave rise to a plethora of big data technologies and systems. The chapter includes sections presenting an overview of current big data technologies and how cloud computing facilitates big data solutions. Furthermore, the chapter presents some of the emerging technologies that enhance big data system capabilities. Finally, the chapter concludes with considerations for organizations wanting to adopt big data technologies and their significance for proactive digital solutions.

Equation 1:

$$O_{\text{fit}} = \frac{C_{\text{model}}}{D_{\text{data}}}$$

Where:

- O_{fit} is the overfitting risk (how likely the model is to overfit).

- C_{model} is the complexity of the AI model (number of parameters, layers in neural networ

- D_{data} is the size of the training data.

11.2.1. Definition and Scope

Big Data One of the constantly referenced works on the phenomenon of big data is given by four authors who argued that big data is "the next frontier for innovation, competition, and productivity", naming it one of the five technologies that will reshape business in 2020. Consequently, whether a phenomenon or economic and technological category, it cannot be denied that big data has come to define the 21st century as the widespread use of the internet and digital technology has given individuals, businesses, and governments access to large volumes of data. There is no general consensus on defining big data. It has been referred to as big data architecture, environment, technology, algorithm, or even simple computing. In general, big data refers to cases where, due to the amount of data of various formats or because of the speed with which data is produced, it is impossible to work with them using traditional methods. The phenomenon of big data is based on the volume, velocity, variety, and veracity of the data.

In terms of its scope, big data is used in many fields. In reality, big data is popular across sectors and industries such as the financial sector, the environmental sector, tourism, e-commerce, healthcare, and the automotive industry because of the versatility of applicable methods. With the ease of access to data and the big data era, many fundamental changes have occurred across the entire system; from healthcare to social science, many enterprises, industries, and research-related activities now depend on big data and artificial intelligence. For example, in the field of nuclear science, big data and AI are used as software packages for data analysis, data mining, and machine learning. These software packages provide insight into the multidimensional datasets and provide predictions using machine learning algorithms.

11.2.2. Key Components and Technologies

Key Components and Technologies. Aside from these fundamental technological tenets, several sub-components are typically associated with Big Data technology. Two primary tools are often discussed as being representative of Big Data: the software framework and the open-source data processing engine. Each of these tools is designed to offer distributed processing capabilities to handle very large datasets across clusters of computers. Versions of data storage systems are the underlying technologies of 'Big Data' systems, albeit in operational and historical guises. In terms of this, it is not uncommon for database solutions (in transactional systems) to consist of implementations based on traditional deployment models alongside Big Data systems within the same organizations for different use cases. Given query-processing models in operational systems, data warehousing has focused on aggregates to increase performance over large, frequently changing datasets.

Fundamentally, the role of analytics technologies is to extract insights from data. The underlying algorithms and methodologies of these have gone through a number of cycles in line with the technological evolution of the time, from early statistical methods up to modern machine learning. At their core, these technologies leverage data mining and statistical techniques to examine datasets against various methodologies and criteria. The insights are typically presented based on reporting and dashboard visualizations within these tools, although they may be combined into larger business intelligence suites. The importance of data integration and processing technologies is fundamental in enabling organizations to develop a cohesive 'Big Data' strategy. The convergence of these two technologies allows organizations to bring multiple data sources together in a single place and gives way to tools and processes to analyze this data as a unified system.

Hardware is less a standalone sub-component than a contributing factor to the decisions surrounding one or more of the key technologies above. The design and architecture of an effective Big Data platform can help an emerging market meet its need for Big Data. Building an infrastructure of servers, networks, and data storage forms the foundation of your Big Data strategy and investment in Big Data. For the Big Data system to be managed, health-checked, and performance-measured, additional management software will be available with each major Big Data product. Hardware and processing come together to undermine a further subset of the Big Data configuration that has been arbitrarily divided into its own area. The analysis of data can be leveraged at the data store level. Can process the seismic data without moving the data through query technology provided at the data store level.

11.3. Generative AI Solutions

Generative AI, otherwise known as generative adversarial networks or autoencoders, goes well beyond traditional AI models, which are primarily discriminative models for problem-solving. While the latter predict outputs based on inputs, generative AI can create original content. Although big data solutions provide greater context based on historical information, generative AI assists with creating context based on historical relevance in a particular context. Generative AI does not construct, produce, or interpret as a consequence of input; instead, it creates from scratch without new input. Generative AI has been used to create art, music, and books; develop photorealistic pictures of human beings that do not exist and CGI that is indistinguishable from film; synthesize text conversation; layout web pages based on natural language input; and design branded products.

Having revolutionized the unstructured domain, generative AI is a highly promising avenue for research and innovation, with significant implications for improving information representation, analytic outcomes, and opportunities within the business. Generative AI operates through deep learning algorithms that use neural networks and, as a set, develop the same model to generate variety and complexity. The researcher trains two networks. The generator makes new content by synthesizing from the training set, and the discriminator is trained to distinguish between real and synthetic data. GANs are, in particular, used to generate fresh, authentic data that may become more data for training other models. Music, art, and poetry are also produced by a diverse group of neural networks. Given the current limitations of novelty, creativity, ethics, and existing practice, more research is necessary in the generative AI domain to determine how generative AI affects society. Similarly, legislation should be developed to guarantee that societal rights and privileges are not inhibited in generative AI technology.

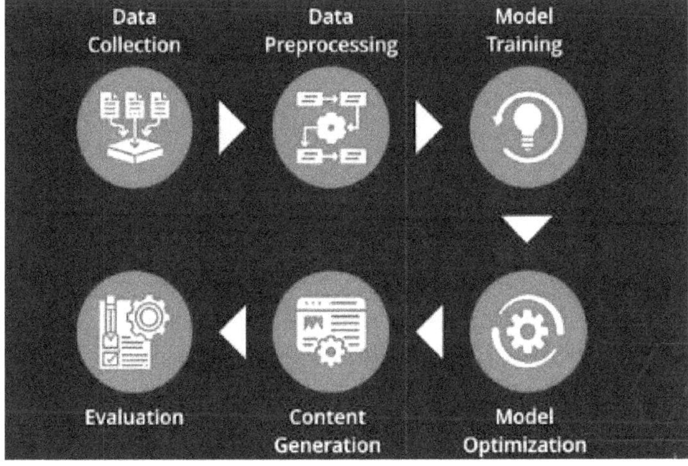

Fig 11.2: Generative AI Solutions

11.3.1. Definition and Applications

Generative AI Today: Definition and Applications AI has been advancing at a remarkable rate. While early generations of AI made great strides in decision-making tasks, AI's capacity for generative creativity has only more recently emerged. Thus, many organizations are not yet familiar with generative AI, its capabilities, and the challenges of commercializing it.

Generative AI represents groundbreaking technological innovation. The term "generative" refers to the process of creating, producing, or bringing forth something, such as new content, new ideas, or new concepts. When applied to AI, generative models refer to machine learning systems that also create new content, ideas, or concepts in collaboration with human users. Due to generative AI's ability to "create" new data that matches—and often expands to—human creativity, its applications are almost limitless. Today's generative AI can assist in creative writing, generate recipes, develop powerful natural language processing models, accelerate drug discovery via molecular generation, and aid sustainable development via human-AI systems that generate new materials. Fields such as art, advertising, education, engineering, entertainment, finance, food science, genomics, materials science, medicine, public health, psychology, ethics, and innovation studies are generating new products and ideas via human-aided and human-AI collaboration. The level to which generative AI systems are able to aid human productivity and the extent of the tasks for which they can do so at a level comparable to or beyond human beings is a matter of ongoing debate. Generative systems that can aid human users by experts in their collaboration are based on a number of technologies, including Generative Adversarial Networks and transformer models. Many practitioners agree that AI can increasingly be involved in creative tasks to a greater and more seamless level. Critics of creating adequate AI systems highlight the likelihood of misuse, such as forgeries, misinformation, and deepfakes. "In the next few years, new collaborations between humans and non-human agents will be explored, both in human-centered professions such as innovation and creativity collaboratives, as well as in other fields such as sociology, ethics, law, computer science, and the arts." "However, the shade of conceptualizing generative AI primarily as an imitation of human-generated artifacts prevents these futures from being probed or researched. Many of generative AI's potentials to become an improved alternative to human-generated products are likewise obscured by these narratives."

11.3.2. Types of Generative AI Models

Generative AI methods can generally be categorized into waveform-based and symbolic AI-based models, depending on how the models handle sound. Generative AI models can also be split into conditional models, designed to generate a specific type of sound, and unconditional models that produce unexpected, new sounds. A number of popular models have been developed within these categories, including Generative Adversarial Networks, Variational Autoencoders, Seq-GAN, and autoregressive models like WaveNet and SampleRNN. Additionally, both GANs and VAEs can also be used to produce conditional audio-generating models.

GANs are a set of two models, a generative model and a discriminative model, that use a zero-sum game framework to learn statistical data distributions. The generator creates new content, such as images or sounds, from an input; when a GAN is applied to sounds, the input might be a sound category and/or a random unstructured noise vector. The discriminator then evaluates how much the generated content deviates from real content from the training set. This process results in the generator improving to the point that the discriminative performance of the discriminator no longer exceeds that of random chance. At this point, the generative model should have learned the distribution of the real content. Despite their ability to generate very sophisticated patterns, GANs are known to suffer from 'mode collapse,' where the GAN generates the same (often trivial) sample many times, and 'training instability.' To address this, a number of GAN variations have also been proposed, including some that train the GANs in a more stable manner. The theoretical functionality of GANs formed the basis of later developments, like VAE-GAN and ACGAN. GAN-based systems have been widely used in art, image, and video generation and editing, even having applications in movie generation and organizations creating models that seamlessly convert photos into animated portraits, and vice versa. In sound, GANs have been applied to a wide range of tasks such as speech enhancement, singing voice generation, and playing technique transfer.

11.4. Challenges in Adopting Big Data Solutions

Big data solutions have garnered significant attention from scholarly literature and the industry. However, many organizations find it challenging to extract potential benefits from these solutions. Governance and data quality are two of the many challenges faced during the adoption of big data analytics. In the context of generative AI, data quality is essential; thus, encoding the requirements, such as privacy and governance at the ingestion point, can make the data repository beneficial for AI applications. Data is a critical asset and a critical success factor for analysis. Even the best analytic techniques would not compensate for poor-quality data. Inadequate data quality can severely impact an organization's analytics initiatives. Effective governance of data can ensure that the organization can overcome this issue.

Due to a lack of high-level tools for the adoption of big data analytics, enterprises with little development expertise are dissuaded.

$$B_{\text{bias}} = \frac{D_{\text{biased}}}{D_{\text{total}}}$$

Where:

- B_{bias} is the bias score (the amount of bias in the model).

- D_{biased} is the amount of biased or unrepresentative data in the training set.

- D_{total} is the total amount of training data.

Equation 2: Ethical and Bias Issues

11.4.1. Data Quality and Governance

Big data initiatives critically rely on the quality of data available. In big data, it is common to employ data from a variety of different sources across departments and organizations. Often, raw data entering a system contains discrepancies, redundancies, and outdated information. Quality issues are often found by users when their results do not conform to their expectations or to the results of a different data analysis process. Common data quality issues comprise duplication, outdated data, incorrect data, inconsistency, incompleteness, and erroneous format. This is why a data governance framework is needed to ensure data quality. Data governance frameworks support the oversight needed to uncover and sustain accurate data.

There are practices to improve data quality. They are: eliminate data entry, include these extra fields in this personnel and resource tracking system, include it in data exports to populate the overtime hours data cube; otherwise, an error will occur; establish usage guidelines that support the specific needs of a variety of data consumers; use software to automatically check data integrity rules and improve the accuracy of data quality by introducing error messages. To minimize data quality issues, data governance efforts should focus on getting better data from diverse sources in the first instance, leading to rectification that is concerned with fixing bad data. The quality of data is dynamic, and if there are not stringent processes in place to monitor changes over decades, and detect and verify data errors, data quality can drop. That is why governance cultures become of paramount importance in disciplines such as data stewardship. Data stewardship comprises people executing documented and approved processes, notified by technology, to enforce governance rules in order to provide quality data. It is based on a holistic approach that builds on an overall governance culture supported by oversight that automated technology provides.

Ensuring data quality across big data initiatives has shown to be the most common challenge. Data stewards need to ensure that good practices and standards are implemented across big data, analytics, and legacy systems. This role can be undertaken by data stewards in organizations that have a holistic approach that aligns with business governance and data stewardship best practices. These organizations typically make use of governance technology to automatically check the quality of the data and will not proceed with data ingestion through big data technology if the quality does not conform with documented quality standards.

11.4.2. Scalability and Infrastructure

For big data systems to be truly successful, they need to be scalable: both to adapt to massive datasets as they grow and to be able to handle an arbitrary number of users each day. An infrastructure that is unable to scale, in the event of a strike of interest, results in one of two scenarios. In the first, it may discourage users from trying again—much like a website that frequently crashes may seldom (if at all) be revisited. Conversely, overly inflated systems result in a significant waste of resources that could otherwise be utilized. Over-provisioning for the off chance of a traffic spike during one small slice of time is an expensive endeavor. The value of using cloud technology, which provides seamless and auto-scaling performance, is significant.

Further, efficiency can be improved by combining different kinds of data into a single database in which analysis and visualization can be performed more easily. Integrating information systems to provide a "single source of truth," or in other words, a data warehouse, offers businesses and analysts accessible data that can be used in real-time reporting, analytics, and intelligence. The plethora of data sources available can make finding a perfect integrative infrastructure difficult. Another challenge organizations face when considering infrastructural improvements is deriving data from data already collected: using it to evaluate how the systems perform, where systemic bottlenecks may occur, and what recommendations (if any) may be taken forth. Integrating modern data analytics into older, inflexible systems is difficult at best. This represents a catch-22 insofar as an infrastructure change is necessary to replace unscalable legacy systems—yet the legacy infrastructure itself prevents them from making that change. Finally, the need for investment in new hardware and software presents a number of challenges of its own, particularly in large organizations where there are many stakeholders. Furthermore, a company may lack the personnel with the technical expertise or the business knowledge to understand and apply the new technology. In many organizations, management boards are not aware of the importance of big data processing.

11.5. Challenges in Adopting Generative AI Solutions

A number of challenges may discourage businesses from adopting AI-generated content solutions. Many experts argue that decisions about regulating and banning AI-generated outputs are driven by legitimate concerns for consumer trust and ethical behavior. AI-generated content may violate copyright, and the intellectual property status of specific problems or outputs created in collaboration with a machine could be unclear. Additionally, without proper governance, AI-generated outputs may reinforce systemic inequalities and power asymmetries through the normalization and marketing of stereotypical assumptions or the erasure of diverse voices already underrepresented in the datasets and training data. Addressing these ethical concerns requires robust regulation and governance. From a legal creative process point of view, another important challenge is the interpretability and explainability of AI-generated solutions.

The interpretability and explainability of machine learning models, particularly of NLP models, have become increasingly debated topics in AI ethics and law, as advancements in AI research have made it difficult to articulate how some solutions are developed. The more stakeholders rely solely on AI to generate new content, the less they will likely be able to engage meaningfully with the justification and explanation process underlying decisions on AI-human collaboration or generated solutions. This has led many AI experts to promote ethical explainability driven by transparency – showcasing not only the abilities but also the limitations of AI, as well as providing transparency on the data, algorithmic techniques, and the application as a substantial tool to "show" and publicly reveal the explainable logic for the decision-making process, strategies, and their source. Fairness and potential conflicts also pose ethical challenges relating to how AI-generated content can be applied and its impacts on human society. Encouraging ongoing public dialogue in these arenas can help identify and mitigate potential issues, develop standards, and build transparency and inclusivity into systems dealing with AI-human-generated content.

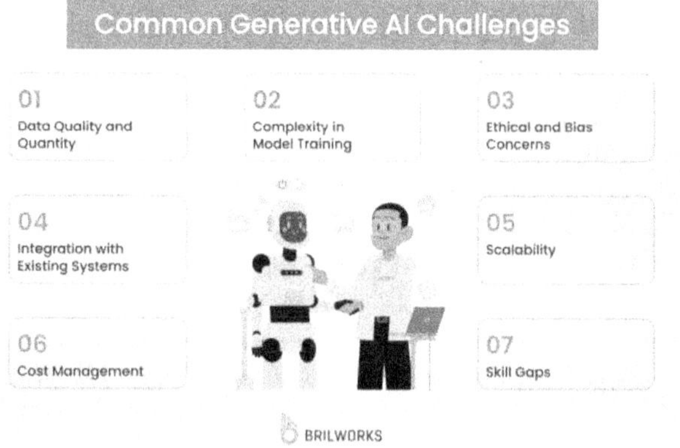

Fig 11.3: Common Generative AI Challenges

11.5.1. Ethical and Legal Concerns

One of the most acute concerns facing machine learning technologies that can autonomously create original content relates to their potential misuse. There is no doubt that the ability to generate highly believable fake materials, such as speech or visual images, can bring about a significant amount of harm: from high-quality fake identity theft to misuse in adversarial attacks to influencing millions through faked news or leaked data. As this technology gains ground in the real world, identifying who has ownership rights for AI-generated materials will also become a non-trivial problem. Although the law traditionally does not recognize the grant of copyright to something created by a machine, it is currently unclear if this will automatically apply to content generated by AI systems used in big data applications.

AI in general is infamous for learning to reproduce human biases and can consequently create content that is biased and discriminatory. Indeed, a study found that for users in the USA, UK, and India, a voice recognition system was less likely to recognize female voices than those of males. Finally, all these AI capabilities need to be governed by a set of regulations. Unfortunately, many use cases are not well understood yet. What that often calls for in the face of multiple and complex causes behind an incident is for developments to be tightly regulated, even if the causes are complex and the new innovation can prove beneficial. For instance, deep learning research in computer vision shows that it should be possible to infer a "passable" amount of privacy through image backgrounds of more than 80 people who received potentially harmful medical procedures. Consent for the procedure may not have been obtained. Cases of this unsolicited intimate visual pattern discovery highlight that discussions and clear guidelines for proper and transparent AI use are necessary. Combined, these concerns introduce a significant challenge to the adoption of AI by industries and the public, whose trust AI should maintain. Ethical dilemmas related to biases in AI are currently a matter of public debate, with one of the first well-known incidents arising in machine learning image classification.

As technologies get deployed more and more widely, this relationship between AI and who is liable for damages is likely to become more important. To tackle these many legal and ethical concerns, there is a large amount of widespread research into new laws and regulations of AI. This is in addition to reinforcing the existing laws that are often broken, like those of cybersecurity and holding both companies harming users via data breaches and the lawmakers themselves accountable to them. Unlike science, all legal and ethical concerns cannot be directly taken into consideration and solved from another part of science, as they have real-world consequences. For each one of the negative scenarios listed, policies must have authority. Providing authority means ensuring that there are necessary mechanisms in place: laws exist to stop people who misbehave, with regulatory frameworks and penalties in place for those who defy them.

11.5.2. Interpretability and Explainability

Interpretability and explainability are two major issues when applying deep learning and, in particular, generative AI models. Many AI models are so complex that the human analyst is not able to properly understand how they work. For many researchers in the field, any AI algorithm is a kind of 'black box' because it is not possible to know what kind of internal operations are carried out to obtain a specific answer. While for traditional AI models, many works have been published for interpreting and explaining how these models work in making a decision or a choice, new solutions must be found to address our lack of knowledge about how deep learning and generative models work internally. Today, one of the main research interests .

Equation 3: Talent Shortage

$$T_{\text{shortage}} = \frac{R_{\text{experts}} - A_{\text{available}}}{R_{\text{experts}}}$$

Where:

- T_{shortage} represents the talent shortage ratio.

- R_{experts} is the required number of skilled professionals (e.g., data scientists, machine learning engineers).

- $A_{\text{available}}$ is the number of qualified professionals available in the job market.

11.6. Conclusion

In conclusion, the integration of solutions at the intersection of big data and generative AI does not simply represent a single technological revolution, but a paradigm with implications on a variety of fronts – from health, bio- and neurotech to private and public security to the media and smart cities – the report of individual aspects could help outline fruitful research subjects themselves. Equipping organizations and individuals to adopt such solutions involves identifying and synthesizing a number of strategic, operational, and normative hurdles that the state of the art cannot currently ignore. The first matter could produce some future research hypotheses: because of the breadth and depth with which new technologies are likely to affect various markets, an analysis conducted in this field should focus on the impact on domains and approaches as a function, e.g., of region, field, size, pressure of internal and external responsibility, etc. The innovative methodological approach is responsible for a high level of innovation. More than fifty in-depth interviews, performed over the course of three years with players in different sectors who intend to face opportunities related to big data and machine learning in a socially responsible manner, starting from the collection, storage, use, and sharing of data. During the research, real barriers and examples of solutions during the research emerged, especially in the healthcare sector. The further development of theory would also require an innovative approach that prevents the creation of a cultural gap between researchers and institutions.

There are substantial strategic hurdles to adopting solutions that require interoperability and familiarity with generative AI on the level of organizations: in most cases, the use of big data and generative AI implicitly requires qualified companies to face cultural shifts, potentially substantial to organizational models and supply chains, which are always closely linked to business strategies. Operational obstacles due to complexity continue to result in critical fears in the intersection of big data and generative AI: an enterprise needs highly specific skill sets to integrate across the field of big data analytics, information architecture, and the whole value chain for machine learning and prevents or solves advanced threats related. One last normative aspect to take care of is the priority of the researchers, companies, and institutions involved in this respect, and it emphasizes the responsibility of individual access and the adoption of solutions for generative AI and big data. The talk goes to how education needs and types of qualifications change to use solutions in populated places. Given the urgency of complying with these challenges, many of the companies surveyed have not actually used generative AI in connection with products or services, developing their resources in the handling of artificial intelligence in unaltered or less subversive techniques. The evolution of the area would also require a deep interdisciplinary confrontation to allow experts from various fields, from policy to business, to join forces, not just researchers. The dialogue must also concern activists and advocates involved in the field, both in the technology sector and in the NGO sector. In addition, there is a need to engage policy makers in considering how these obstacles justify the need and adoption, and how policy can contribute to a responsible adoption through the development of qualifications.

11.6.1. Future Trends

The recent growth of big data and advancements in generative AI, in particular, have provided useful solutions for many business applications. Nevertheless, their future constructs are not yet well sketched. Several developments are, however, expected in the future, which is speculated to shape the big data environment and generative AI for likelihood. These changes will herald improvements in current technologies, enabling their wider adoption in emerging areas and helping in their sustainable development. Technology is innovating very rapidly towards more complicated quantum computing. This quantum computing can standardize all the big data deployed in organizations. At the same time, machine learning algorithms are also improvising gradually with the AutoAI invention. All these practices need regulation to guard against misuse and better user acceptance. Thus, regulation is predicted to be catered to keep pace with technological advancements. Enterprises and governments globally are expected to prioritize business ethics, especially in AI due to the expanding AI community in society. Individuals are foresighted to trust and prefer to use those machines that are labeled with any recommended ethical seals for high-quality goods and services. As per the suggestions and listings, the technology adoption takes place. Moreover, the world is changing according to social and economic images that reduce technology indifference to almost zero. Thus, there will be an induction of the Internet of Things and connected devices where every device is predicted to be connected. Big data analytics will play a crucial role in predicting customers' purchasing preferences for forthcoming Internet of Things products. An increase in demand for awards of big data and generative policies has been observed. Mostly, the regulatory bodies ask for the need for the formation of new amendments in their regulatory framework. Artificial intelligence can be useful to explore unexplored areas of outer space. It is expected that drones, the internet, and the cloud have stabilized to support such initiatives. In the future, big data and machine learning will converge and create a narrower stream for big data and generative AI permissions.

This will lead to the creation of innovations in this domain. Thus, an increase in R&D has been forecasted to be directed towards unforeseen challenges in this technology fusion.

References

[1]Dastin, J. (2019). AI for business leaders: Transformative strategies. HarperCollins.

[2]Yang, Y., & Zhou, H. (2022). The competitive advantage of using big data for business transformation. International Journal of Management, 31(3), 100-115.

[3]Alvarado, S., & Wang, X. (2020). Implementing big data and AI for business scalability. Journal of Business Insights, 5(1), 34-45.

[4]Madsen, A., & White, A. (2021). Machine learning and AI for business success. Oxford University Press.

[5]Ghosh, R., & Rehman, M. (2022). Data-driven decision-making: A path to organizational growth. Journal of Decision Sciences, 31(2), 122-135.

12

The Future of Organizational Success: Big Data, Generative AI, and Beyond

12.1. Introduction

'A generation from now,' three leading technology and operations executives observe, 'the use of power by modern organizations will have become nearly perfectly transparent, as Big Data ensures that every action is recorded, filed, and analyzed in real-time, and as organizations are guided directly by generative artificial intelligence to ensure that production runs exactly to anticipated demand and that decisions are made to maximize customer experiences and organizational returns.' They go on to explore the wider implications for the future of organizational operational practices and decision-making. While drawing attention to the potential challenges faced by practitioners, they argue that human capabilities and institutional architectures will evolve to keep pace with the radical change in underlying technologies witnessed today. 'The only way to guarantee that your organization has a future in such a world,' they conclude, 'is to be the organization committing to realizing it.'

Unfortunately, the obstacles are more stubborn than their formulants let on. Two distinct challenges interfere with the future that they envision—and therefore the capability of the people, institutions, and organizational forms they inhabit to realize such a world. The first hurdle is organizational. Many existing organizational structures bear no resemblance to the collection of 'highly collaborative, creative, intuitive, and thoughtful participants' in 'information-rich marketplaces' that the authors hypothesize occupy their worlds of 'transparency and projected generativity.' The second hurdle is social—a matter of strings-attached determination. While the authors can claim optimistically that, in their future world, 'the fundamental measure of success will be your capacity to create a worthwhile future through your worthwhile decisions and other material and immaterial effects,' they elide the fact of no longer cutting decisions loose from what could be called the question of their worth: for whom?

12.1.1. Background and Significance

The emergence of the digital age heralded significant shifts in some of the most foundational capabilities of organizational infrastructure. One of the most visible of those capabilities is the evolving nature of data and metadata processing. Up until the 2000s, shared organizational data processing that would now be called "Big Data" was handled exclusively by mainframe and later distributed systems that kept a small range of data warm and processed it frequently in an organizational data warehouse. While these sufficed for the storage and processing needs of most, parts of the civilian and military communities increasingly encountered business challenges that led to the need for systems that could manage data in dozens to hundreds of virtual computers. The price-performance benefits of cloud computing have never been questioned, and since ideation, it has been identified as the future of computational infrastructure.

Fig 12.1: The Future in the Era of Generative AI

12.1.2. Research Aim and Objectives

This research aims to craft a narrative that can account for recent leaps in technological advancements, namely Big Data and Generative AI, and that has the potential to transcend from mere good management practice to shape commercial possibilities leading to project advances and successes. In short, it argues that Big Data and Generative AI drive organizational success now and in the future. We explore these aims in full throughout this current research study. The objectives of the research study are to: - Explore practical applications of Big Data and Generative AI that can lead to better projects and to ask how the capabilities manifest through day-to-day practices and discourses. - Unpack the implications of organizational adoptions of these technologies for the range of stakeholders who participate in project-related activities, including craft and construction labor, sales and marketing, and investor relations. Importantly, we underline that we do not seek to merely report on the experiences of organizations' Big Data and Generative AI journey. Instead, we aim to conclude this embryonic empirical study with a set of fairly weighty propositions, or organizational 'Big Statement,' that can begin to offer guidelines or tactics for acting upon our observations and analysis. It is only through the conduct of new empirical research that we may derive meaningful insights into Big Data

12.2. Big Data and Organizational Success

The vast majority of contemporary organizations use data of any kind to some extent for both strategic decision-making, aiming at maintaining or improving their competitive advantage, and for improving operational processes. This data includes but is not limited to, customer data, market data like demand forecasts or expected outcomes of marketing strategies, productivity metrics, performance reports, financial statements, relevant institutions, etc. Besides quantitative and qualitative data, some advanced techniques and databases allow managers and researchers to ingest, store, and analyze data such as texts produced in social media, recordings of the environment, and automatic natural language processing, such as images, sounds, and videos. Indeed, big data and data analytics have been progressively adopted by organizations in diverse sectors and industries, to analyze consumer behavior, and market trends, design better products, and compare offers to predict marketing impacts, as well as to design efficient information-based management and production strategies. However, one should keep in mind that handling huge amounts of data can be challenging. For instance, there are some important concerns about the standardization and quality of the information, as well as data storage. For instance, companies lack data scientists or data management expertise, as well as equipment of high computing performance, available to process this data and extract interesting patterns and valuable information. In addition, some industries are data-poor compared to others, leading to unequal opportunities in terms of applying data-driven technologies and processes. Nonetheless, it is well known that becoming a data-driven operation can be a source of competitive advantage as well as open a door for radical innovation in managing, distributing, and using energy.

Equation 1: Organizational Performance and Big Data

$$P - f(Q, V, E)$$

Where:

- P is the organizational performance or success.

- Q is the quality of data (accuracy, relevance, timeliness).

- V is the volume of data (more data can lead to better insights).

- E is the effectiveness of data processing (e.g., data analytics, insights extraction).

12.2.1. Definition and Scope of Big Data

In recent times, we have witnessed an explosion in digital data, with projections indicating that global digital data will reach 180 zettabytes by 2025, up from 4.4 zettabytes in 2013. The volume alone in such scenarios is significant. Building on this premise, this section establishes the definition and scope of Big Data, detailing the dimensions that delineate it from small data sets. The section further identifies technological advancements that have led to the accelerated adoption of Big Data solutions in organizations. In particular, key innovations underlying the rise of Big Data analytics include the conception and development of large-scale data storage and processing infrastructures, semantically rich data-exchange formats, NoSQL databases, cloud database services linked to data storage environments, and distributed computing, which have diffused rapidly across social, economic, and governance contexts, generating new business models, practices, and capabilities across the private, public, and non-profit sectors. It also delineates the key differences between Big Data and more traditional forms of business data and information, including details on the volume, velocity, variety, and veracity of Big Data. These dimensions are extremely important because they fundamentally alter how data should be collected, stored, processed, and analyzed in organizations.

While there remains no consensus among scholars, industry experts, and practitioners regarding a single, unifying definition of Big Data, all tend to agree that it can be described in terms of five key characteristics. From over 90 definitions of Big Data proposed by different researchers, the use of five different terms to differentiate the concept from that of "small data," ranging from "volume of the data set" and the "extreme nature of the data" in terms of "size, complexity, and variety"; the "variety and density of the data" involved and "the need to manage and analyze it," as well as the operations associated with "the ability to capture, store, search, share, analyze, and visualize Big Data" that adapt to the changing contexts. Some conceptualizations take a stronger focus on defining data characteristics, while others focus on the potential benefits that can be derived from the use of these new types of data. Most definitions conceptualize Big Data through a combination of both data characteristics and the potential impact that the data could have on the generation of insights or actions.

12.2.2. Applications of Big Data in Organizations

Analyzing data to gain new insights can be applied to many functions within an organization. Often, the most visible areas where data analytics can be applied are in marketing. Tracking consumer behavior and social media comments can provide a wealth of data and actionable insights. Big data applications for marketing range from advertising effectiveness to product design, customer segmentation, and understanding customer sentiment. Data can also be used to improve customer service. Big data tools can help to track customer satisfaction as well as track customer complaints and concerns, leading to improved customer service. Organizations also use big data as part of their operations. Airlines use historical data on weather patterns and customer no-shows to predict demand and dynamically price tickets. By using data, they can get the best price for each seat sold, leading to increased revenue for the airline.

Data analytics can also improve decision-making. Executives who want to be data-driven are also more likely to be able to solve complex problems and understand risk, as well as be more able to identify new business opportunities. This way, big data helps to improve decision-making and increase levels of innovation in organizations by using both predictive analytics and deep learning or generative artificial intelligence to see patterns in data that would be difficult or impossible for a human to analyze. Big data applications such as this can also help to develop new products and processes that can offer a potential source of competitive advantage. To remain competitive, more companies are using big data applications. This allows them to gain a competitive advantage and outperform their rivals. Many industries can offer examples of big data use, especially in the digital space, but also in industries like insurance, food production, retail, pharmaceuticals, and media, and the influence of the public sector is coming to light. Companies use big data to prevent fraud, develop search engines, and improve case-based analysis of medical information. Companies use big data applications to improve customer satisfaction and decrease customer churn. Despite the numerous advantages of using big data, there are also some challenges. Privacy and data protection can be a major barrier to use, and organizations may need to ensure they are using data that they have the right to use. Regulatory compliance with data protection laws and privacy rights may also be barriers to using big data. Companies must ensure they develop robust systems, processes, and governance and carefully implement data management solutions to prevent potential misuse of data.

12.3. Generative AI and its Impact

Before we discuss the specifics of artificial intelligence in general, and generative AI in particular, it is important to position it within the evolving technology landscape that currently includes the similarly trendy big data and machine learning. Perhaps the most differentiating element of AI that sets it apart from this landscape is that while big data focuses on accumulating and analyzing large datasets and machine learning focuses on finding patterns in the data, AI aims to predict future data. Generative AI goes even further by predicting novel data, which is data or content that is very different from the examples it was trained on.

Generative AI relies on the use of machine learning constructs called neural networks, which are models that have a very high capacity to learn from large amounts of data. When trained on data, they can then generate new data that are not exact copies of the originals but maintain the original data's traits. The implications of this are manifold, and they can be deployed in pattern recognition and product development, content creation and simulation, data imputation or fault detection, or automating tasks and decision-making. The novelty of the generated artifacts can stimulate team creativity and increase the rates of hypothesis generation, and using it for data systematic exploration can be similarly beneficial when seeking to acquire new knowledge about the search space from which data came. It is indeed difficult to overestimate the potential impact of generative AI applications and their increasing sophistication on the technological capabilities of organizations.

One of the challenges with generative AI, however, is its potential to produce outputs that are unethical, discriminatory, or undesirable. Indeed, it is not infrequent to find AI programs that have been trained on data that is distorted towards minority groups to produce outputs that also discriminate against these groups. The mere act of deciding which instructions to give to the AI system can have implications on the way that system learns and the content it creates. Given that there are not always best practices for every ethical situation, important ethical tasks include understanding the possible consequences of deploying a generative AI system on people's privacy or civil rights and weighing these against the potential benefits of using such technology. Therefore, as with any AI implementation, it is also important that the deployment of generative AI be closely aligned with an organization's strategy and goals.

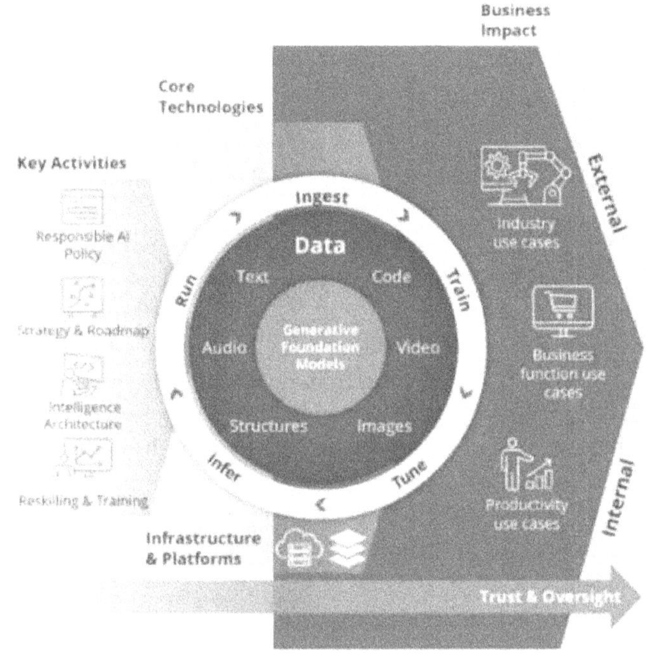

Fig 12.2: Generative AI: The Path to Impact

12.3.1. Understanding Generative AI

Generative AI is a powerful solution in that it can create and produce something that wasn't there beforehand. So, instead of an AI that just performs tasks right or delivers something available, a generative approach seeks to drive an AI into a creative role. The tools, technologies, and services that make this possible are offering opportunities for all industries to completely change their approaches. In a little while, different

194

pipelines will be created and will be doing things different than today. Technologies that make generative AI are based on leveraging a creative adversarial network. They feed a dataset into a creativity algorithm and, using those algorithms, create new outputs that are not based on the training set. Some of these algorithms include using deep learning. The training data has to be designed and constructed in a way that the generative AI will find it easy to manipulate and generate new pieces or designs.

12.3.2. Benefits and Challenges in Organizational Context

In recent years, the commercial uses of generative AI have become plentiful, from functioning as personal assistants in our phones and smart speakers to generating innovative musical compositions or artworks. This has relevance across various organizations. In terms of efficiency and innovation opportunities, automating tasks using generative AI could create enough time to enable people to prioritize work that demands softer, emotional cognitive capacities, such as empathy. It could offer organizations new products, processes, or offerings because people are spending more time on innovative and creative capacities. It could also fundamentally inform insights and product predictions through the possibility of moving from back-testing simulations to forward experimentation. In turn, these insights enable better and faster decisions. Another potential benefit of AI applied to organizations includes operational transformation and excellence. Consequently, AI would also improve decision-making processes within the operation of the organization by automating tasks and pulling together information across the system to inform the decision. Operational benefits would come from automating repetitive, lower-order work and deploying generative AI systems that respond to the merits of context in real-time. Implementing generative AI in an organizational context also generates considerations or costs for the organization and the people within it, in addition to the ethical implications that urgently require the development of enabling frameworks. Significant cost considerations in the implementation of generative AI range from financial and technological investments to time, in ensuring the AI system fits the needs of the organization. These costs do not only surface in the implementation of generative AI but there are also ongoing costs. These include maintenance and updating of associated technology, as well as re-skilling, re-training, or up-skilling of existing employees, or finding human talent that stands the chance of being displaced to up-skill from external sources. Although the profession is divided on whether it will displace job roles shortly, as most office workers are also teachers, healthcare support staff, or involved in predictive data analytics in contrast to their current roles, there are also theoretical debates fundamentally contrasting generative AI with deskilling. Regulation and control of AI in an organization go beyond economic issues. Companies also need to consider potential ethical concerns about AI-generated content, and how these systems are trained and deployed in organizations could perpetuate existing biases. Realizing the benefits of generative AI requires balancing organizational and regulatory requirements for ethical, theoretical, and technological appropriateness. These considerations are critical for the organization when integrating technologies such as generative AI into the broader organizational strategy.

12.4. Integration of Big Data and Generative AI

The integration of Big Data and Generative AI creates new data and provides a complementary enhancement of benefits. It potentially has the same potential for development as the integration of Inductive AI into BI. The processes of an organization can improve over time by learning from its produced data and adapting its outputs to match the quality dimensions required to receive specific benefits from those outputs. In this sense, Big Data might help improve the quality of the outputs of Generative AI.

When Generative AIs leverage Big Data, they can learn what would be "most relevant" or interesting for certain values of evidence. Another reason why managers of organizations may want to employ Generative AI that leverages Big Data is when there is evidence for that co-adaptive system. Large corporations have been developing business models and algorithms based on those models to control data sources and predict what types of information or entertainment will become popular in the future, leveraging a co-adaptive AI, which generates data through its actions and learns precise feedback from that data. Especially demanding is the effective understanding of the relationship between the AI components producing or making decisions from Generative AI and any BI. Here, we focus on Generative AI since it has been considered to hold probably the strongest potential to be part of the core paradigm and to provide "smart" support in strategic management and BI. While the integration of Generative AI and BI has received little attention, we provided an initial exploration of this focus and elaborated on its primary strategic implications. This study had a qualitative, theoretical-empirical case research approach. Based on existing literature, the paper presents a conceptual framework. This paper argues that Generative AI could help bridge actual strategic IT issues by adding data in BI functions and making data-based results more actionable, thus potentially increasing efficiency and effectiveness in both BI and organizational strategy. In doing so, it makes an important contribution to BI and strategic IT management research in general.

Equation 2: Generative AI Impact on Innovation

12.4.1. Synergies and Complementarities

This chapter will explore one aspect of the future of organizations, namely, the dynamic synergies and complementarities that Big Data and Generative AI share. To explain how they may be two sides of the same coin, we will highlight the various ways in which Generative AI uses Big Data as both inputs and outputs. There are several processes at work behind the synergy between Big Data and Generative AI. More specifically, Big Data often serves as the input to Generative AI, which is then trained to produce the desired outputs. First of all, Big Data can serve as a valuable resource to train these Generative AI models, making them as accurate as possible based on the database they have carefully developed. Second, Generative AI is also playing a growing role in the world of Big Data by improving the way data is collected to be more accurate and relevant to the analysis at hand.

Moreover, Generative AI enables Big Data with predictive insights on what is going to happen shortly. These complementarities between Big Data and Generative AI lead to a new research question about the potential of combining Big Data and advanced analytical approaches that rely on Generative AI results, and in the process create feedback loops that refine both. This is fundamentally a techno-managerial question, which concerns the exploration of technological

$$I = f(C, S, U)$$

Where:

- C is the creativity and novelty brought by the AI (e.g., new ideas, designs, solutions).

- S is the speed at which AI-driven processes can be implemented (e.g., reducing time to market).

- U is the level of customization that AI allows (e.g., personalized products, tailored services).

complements and substitutes. There is a historical corollary between advances in computing and advances in managerial skills in the employment of new technologies. The most illustrative example would be the seminal paper concerning yet another computing innovation, the management implications of utilizing expert systems for knowledge management within organizations. In this case, expert systems were thought to take over what was previously a human skill, and diagnosis, and thus allow humans to focus on other management tasks. What is certain in the development of Generative AI is that Big Data will feed into these systems, and AI will make the results of Big Data collection more meaningful. A few organizations have started to exploit the synergies and complementarities between Big Data and Generative AI to enhance their performance. It is still early to have definitive examples or create a typology of practices, as the potential convergence of Big Data and Generative AI is something that has only recently begun to be undertaken. However, the examples allow a first reading of the possible advantages and potentialities that highlight how innovation is moving in the direction of the integration of all the technological tools available in a scenario that has already transitioned from an information society to a liquid society where data flows.

12.4.2. Case Studies

The four child pages in this Case Studies section exemplify a few successful applications of combining generative AI and big data in organizations and industries. These four stories span different industries and are separated by the technology that is the key feature of integration and feature a brief synopsis, lesson learned, and breakdown of the problem, methods, and outcomes approached by each industry. The section will make use of general analytics in light of example applications in big data and AI, as well as lessons learned and suggestions previously mentioned to provide a condensed part about privacy and policy. This could offer a prominent introduction to the stigma associated with using big data to an organization's advantage. This page may focus on ethics and regulations and point to specific examples in the following segment using any of the case studies.

The best practices regarding the real-world application of these technologies can be garnered by studying organizations currently at the forefront of these approaches. Each best practice is based on a specific case study that exemplifies the technology's real-world potential, as applied in a data-intensive organizational strategy. For instance, one organization utilized big data analytics in selling inventory management software, and by doing so was able to reach many of the thousands of challenging white papers online, cutting through the white noise of the internet to connect with a new wave of self-selected buyers. Another organization utilized AI as a prime aspect of their app and website: they employed big data analytics in price optimization and to account for means, but the additional cutting-edge component is their use of generative AI to further supplement the means necessary. The section is summarized in a table and graphed in a figure.

12.5. Future Directions and Implications

Based on the advancements that we have seen from each new technology embraced in the investment industry, we anticipate that more capabilities will be built on the foundations of big data and generative AI. This could eventually include the ability to issue dramatic simulations of extreme future environments that decision-makers might not have anticipated or that differ so greatly from the present that they are not currently relevant. The information environment today is moving very quickly due to the use of AI, and that, too, is rapidly advancing. Investment teams that fail to continuously update their efforts will eventually reach the point where they consider the latest information in their system is no longer differentiating. They will no longer be able to offer an advantage over other current investment practitioners. This has profound implications for the industry, particularly as it affects needed research and analysis skills, team assessments, and business cultures. Our advice to stay ahead of the times is to explore and enjoy generative AI while continuing to look out for its successor. While the big growth drivers are easily understood, trends show that the landscape continues to change and move. It is impossible to anticipate what will power these changes. AR and IoT may become key and contribute to the growth of product development. More industries and products may also be involved. We encourage organizations to become more agile in their capacities to act on their drivers. Furthermore, personal and organizational commitment to learning is increasingly important. Should companies collaborate to share in looking for new options going logically and beyond logical interest? These are uncharted waters and open to new possibilities for different organizations. Ethical concerns for all of these opportunities are clear. All have strong potential positive impacts on quality of life, but deployment should be carefully thought through. If we consider these anticipated directions, we need to continue their development and indeed accelerate as necessary.

12.5.1. Emerging Technologies Beyond Big Data and Generative AI

Beyond big data and generative AI, several new technologies have recently emerged. I present a working space and highlight several of these emerging technologies, including automation bots, blockchain, quantum computing, conversational agents, and digital assistants. Each technology has the potential to transform processes, products, or services in different sectors of the economy. For example, automation bots stand to drastically redefine processes across finance, human resource management, and beyond. Many functions will likely be performed by automation bots. Finance, accounting, customer service management, and human resources come immediately to mind. At the same time, the adoption of automation bots and other emerging technologies by early movers suggests that, although potential can be exciting and enticing, the realities of

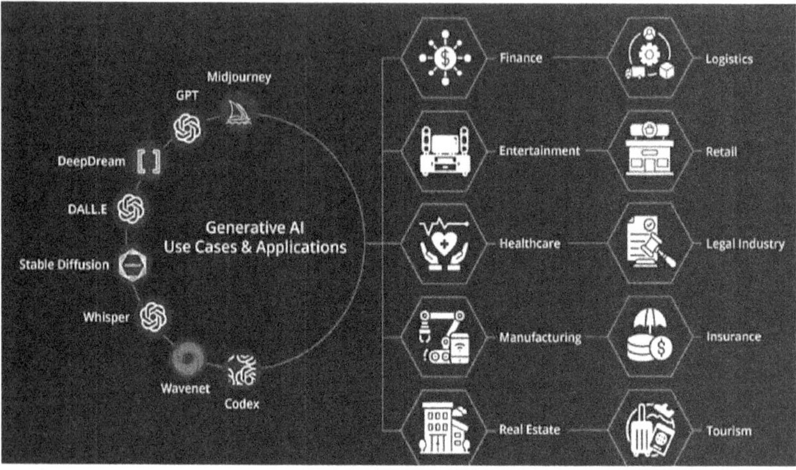

implementation can be more complicated than they appear.

While relatively few organizations have used blockchain in their operations, firms and industries are beginning to explore its potential. Some of the most frequent use cases for blockchain involve supply chain management and provenance, forging transparent processes and quality standards. One way we came to understand the potential of emergent technologies in the present was to consider the implications for sectors of the economy: from how creative industries to public sector organizations to manufacturing companies will change their products, services, and processes in response to new developments.

Fig 12.3: TRENDS Research & Advisory - The Rise of Generative AI

12.5.2. Ethical and Regulatory Considerations

Because the technology of big data and AI can connect vast amounts of personal information directly to individuals, there are a host of issues related to who owns the data, security, identity protection, patent rights, the protection of sensitive intellectual property, and the creation of equitable algorithms that advance human welfare and well-being. Mere regulation and enforcement efforts by the government and self-regulation by organizations are not enough to guarantee human rights. Both society and the organization must play a part. The latter can do little more than ensure that algorithms, data use, and subsequent AI applications are based on accepted principles, guidelines, and ethical standards. In essence, the more we learn about ethical AI, the less clear we are about its legitimate uses and potential to disrupt human labor, privacy, or personal safety and security. Hence, the challenge facing organizational leaders is to strike a balance between the ethical dilemmas of using big data and AI and the decision to select their

$$G - g(DDM, I, M)$$

Where:

- G is business growth (revenues, market share, profitability).

- DDM is data-driven decision-making (how much the organization relies on data for decisions).

- I is the innovation fostered by generative AI and data analysis.

- M is the market adaptability (the ability to respond to trends, customer needs, and competitor actions).

applications. Organizational leaders must ask themselves whether it is possible to use new big data and AI technologies for good, with the current talent, legal framework, and regulations they possess. To make our point straightforward, organizations must work proactively with policymakers and citizens to ensure that the development of AI is guided by a clear vision of responsible, shared innovation and that the transformation supports the development of fair governance arrangements.

Equation 3: Data-Driven Decision Making and Business Growth

12.6. Conclusion

In the beginning, we mentioned that the sheer volume of data available for analysis continues to grow at an exponential rate. In the final section, we discuss an innovation that has the potential to usher in a new data revolution for organizations and may eventually make large datasets obsolete: generative AI. Generative AI can leverage limited data, making predictions and providing accurate insights at the individual level. How organizations integrate these new capabilities into their strategic orientations – with significant investments in human and data science resources – will ultimately determine their operational efficiency and future path of development. Moving beyond curve-fitting outcomes, our final aim in writing this essay was to provide some advice for addressing the challenges and obstacles involved in setting the correct path ahead for technological innovation. The essays in this special edition highlight many of the challenges faced by organizations. With the rapid change of technological capabilities and the constant pressure for businesses to outperform one another in a world with limited resources, battling to keep up is present in a large number of technologies. Thus, finding investments in technologies with a return of competitive advantage for a business represents a key managerial challenge. Moreover, ethical problems deeply intertwine with these new investments, and any investments in future trends will need a cautious eye on the ethical consequences. The evidence produced in front of us illustrates a compelling suggestion that managers and policymakers cannot afford to ignore. The future growth and development of any firm will be strongly rooted in the strategic use of technology. Attention needs to be paid in the present to develop and maintain the right team members and develop the necessary resources both now and in the future. If the basics of organizations aren't attended to in the present, they may simply be behind the curve later on. The time for action is now.

12.6.1. Future Trends

Due to the unprecedented disruption that this multi-billion dollar industry faces, it is almost impossible to anticipate future trends. Yet some have named the most significant ones. They mention the rise of real-time data analytics with data unification platforms because they enable businesses to probe and analyze web interactions in real-time or almost in real-time. Data that was previously thought of as 'company-only' had no means of being analyzed in the field broader than the company's interests. As more data unifies and becomes available, the need for personalization will become an integral part of any business model and a key strategy. A related trend would be an increase in the sophistication and uptake of big data analytics driving smarter business intelligence around potential criminal behavior.

Connected with data and data science, generative AI will expand the technology 'collection,' and it will become increasingly interoperable. There will be no unique capability to access technology or a prevailing set of algorithms. Combined with building data alliances, technology organizations will know how to interconnect to tap into one another's sources, providing a common and dynamic 'sieve' through which to parse that information for warning indicators. Thus, socio-economic constraints will come into play; they will largely shape the way technologies are adopted and funded more than the way they evolve. National security threats and individual financial advancement are unlikely to aid technologies in gaining market footholds. Political and social priorities should become the next drivers to capture the strategic innovation technology space. Thus, those businesses that are looking smart should already start thinking about trends in politics and legislation. In order not to find themselves behind the technology curve, top management should plant seeds of innovative techno-culture within the organization. For longer-term adoption and competitive advantage, the use of technological trends corporate-wide, a strategic investment, and the establishment of preferable technology alliances are recommendable. Organizational goals to reach long-term technology advances should be realized before competitors expend their full phase of rapid technological and organizational changes.

References

[1]Kuo, Y., & Lee, K. (2020). AI and big data: Reshaping business models for the future. Journal of Business Development, 42(5), 118-130.

[2]Lee, J. C., & Park, S. (2019). Big data and generative AI: Transformative technologies in business. Journal of Digital Strategy, 7(4), 254-267.

[3]Sharma, S., & Kumar, R. (2021). Harnessing the power of AI for scalable organizational growth. Springer.

[4]Li, F., & Yu, Z. (2021). AI-enabled data analytics for sustainable business growth. Journal of Sustainable Business, 6(1), 15-28.

[5]Lee, J. (2021). The strategic role of AI in business growth and innovation. McGraw-Hill.

9 7 9 8 8 9 6 9 1 3 6 1 0